DUANE BRADLEY was serving as roving reporter for her local newspaper in a small Missouri town at the age of 12. Later she worked on California newspapers for a number of years and is now Henniker correspondent for the *Monitor,* Concord, New Hampshire. She herself exemplifies the qualities of a good newspaper man (or woman) set forth in this book—an active curiosity, a strong faith in the democratic process, and a belief in the right of the people to know the facts about whatever concerns them.

Duane Bradley (Mrs. George Sanborn in private life) was born in Iowa and spent her childhood in the rich farming areas of that state and Missouri, eventually moving to southern California.

During World War II she and her family saw more of the United States as her husband's army service assignments took them to Washington, Rhode Island, and Delaware. By the end of the war they had settled in the small New Hampshire town where they now live and from which her husband's family originally came. Her early interest in writing expressed itself in short verses and stories, and by her teens she had won a prize in a national short story contest. She has published eight other books for young people.

Her first book for Van Nostrand's juvenile list was *Electing a President,* which was selected by the U. S. Information Agency for publication in Korean.

THE NEWSPAPER—
ITS PLACE IN A DEMOCRACY

The Newspaper—
Its Place in a Democracy

DUANE BRADLEY

D. VAN NOSTRAND COMPANY, INC.
Princeton, New Jersey
Toronto · New York · London

D. VAN NOSTRAND COMPANY, INC.
120 Alexander St., Princeton, New Jersey (*Principal office*)
24 West 40th Street, New York 18, New York
D. Van Nostrand Company, Ltd.
358, Kensington High Street, London, W.14, England
D. Van Nostrand Company (Canada), Ltd.
25 Hollinger Road, Toronto 16, Canada

Published simultaneously in Canada by
D. Van Nostrand Company (Canada), Ltd.

Library of Congress Catalog Card No. 65-25535

FIRST PRINTING OCTOBER 1965,
SECOND PRINTING OCTOBER 1966

PRINTED IN THE UNITED STATES OF AMERICA

FOR GEORGE HORNELL MORRIS

POET, TEACHER, PHILOSOPHER &

GENTLEMAN OF THE PRESS

Contents

****

THE NEWSPAPER—

ITS PLACE IN A DEMOCRACY

1. What Is a Free Press?

"Give me the liberty to know, to utter, and to argue freely according to conscience, above all liberties." John Milton, *Areopagitica*, 1644.

****

Device used on Holt's *New York Journal* after the meeting of the first Congress.

THE WORD "NEWS-PAPER" would seem to mean a paper containing news. We are provided with so much news, so easily, that we do not realize exactly what it means to us. We often criticize newspapers for being inaccurate and inefficient, but we expect them to tell us about everything of importance that is happening in the world.

This national characteristic has helped to create American newspapers as we know them. We were one of the first peoples in the world to believe that we are entitled to know the whole truth about everything that interests us. We still believe that the sheets of newsprint we buy for less than the cost of a loaf of bread or a subway token should give us a complete, accurate, and unbiased account of the condition and happenings of the world.

The freedom of newspapers to print the news is often called "the first freedom." When news and freedom become synonymous, then news is more than printed sheets of paper, more than accounts of events, and more than an immediate report of what is happening. The free and unhampered printing and distribution of news provides a forum in which truth may become clear.

If you have ever followed the progress of a political campaign in the newspapers, you have seen this happen. Each candidate makes speeches and gives interviews in which he expresses his opinions of national and international affairs. Other members of each party join in, telling what is good about themselves and wrong about their opponents. Editorials make their appearance to tell what position the newspaper takes. Letters to the editor tell what the readers think about the candidates, the campaign, the issues, and the opinion of the newspaper. Soon the air is thick with dissension and discussion, and it may seem that all is confusion. What is actually happening is that the newspapers are helping the truth to emerge by printing so many viewpoints and so many different opinions.

The mere existence of newspapers does not guarantee freedom to anyone. There were newspapers in the world before our concept of democracy was born, and there are newspapers today in almost every country, regardless of its type of government. Russia, with a totalitarian government, guarantees its people freedom of the press. The words mean something entirely different to that country than they mean to us.

Many American newspapers have a slogan or motto which is printed daily on their mastheads. Two of the most popular are the Biblical verse, "And ye shall know the truth, and the truth shall make you free," and the quotation from Daniel Webster, "There is nothing so powerful as the truth." Since the news is gathered, written, edited, and printed by human beings with various flaws and weaknesses, it is doubtful if any newspaper always lives up completely to its high ideals. We cannot expect, therefore, that any edition of any newspaper contains all of the truth about anything. We do believe that as long as many different newspapers produced by many people with varying abilities and viewpoints exist, the truth will eventually become clear to us. Our freedom of the press does not mean that newspapers are free to exist, but that they are free to learn and publish all of the news. It is here that our papers differ from those in totalitarian countries.

There are three ways in which newspapers attempt to make their news truthful. They are accuracy, completeness, and controversy.

Accuracy is impressed on every cub reporter. Every detail of the five elements of the news story—who, what, when, where and how —must be correct. The names of those concerned must be complete (with middle initial) and properly spelled, with an identifying tag if it helps to place the story in perspective. John W. Jones who is arrested for speeding makes a minor story—John W. Jones, governor of the state, arrested for speeding, makes a more important story. *What* has happened is to be written in exact terms, *where* by a definite description, *when* in terms of hour, day, and month, and *how* in detail.

The second element in the search for truth is completeness of coverage. A newspaper controlled by the government may be perfectly free to print stories about good things done by the government but not to report mistakes or failures or injustices. The problem with American newspapers is more subtle, and more acute. The very freedom of our press holds its own special dangers.

Suppose that you were the editor of a paper which had helped to oust a corrupt state government and to elect an honest and upright man, as governor. A larger and more powerful paper than yours, and your deadly rival, wants to unseat him and restore the former group to power. You know the rival candidate to be a man of no integrity who will impoverish the state.

One of your reporters has learned from a policeman in a very small town that your candidate has been involved in a traffic accident and will have to face charges in court. Only you, the reporter, the policeman, and the judge of the small town court know about the incident, and the others have agreed to keep it secret. (Police and court news are in the public domain and *may* be printed, but the law does not require that they be reported to the papers. Newspapers are free to get such news if they wish, but it is often not used, especially in small towns, because few people involved with the law care to have it made public.) You know that publishing the

5

story will harm your candidate and your attempt to reform state politics. If you do not print it, probably no one will ever know about it. What do you do?

In another instance, you may learn that a youngster has been attacked by thugs in a public park in your city. When you ask the police for details they ask you not to print the story because secrecy will help them detect and arrest the offenders. They plan a stake-out in the park to trap the thugs and it will fail if the incident is made known. It is your belief that parents should know the park is unsafe, but you do not want to hamper the forces of law and order. What do you do?

As editor, you know that you must sell advertising in order to exist. The son of one of your largest advertisers is arrested on a drunk-driving charge and you are requested to keep the story out of your paper. There is no competing newspaper or radio station in your area that covers such news so you cannot tell the advertiser that the story will be made public whether you print it or not. If he withdraws his account, you will not be able to pay your bills. The chief of police has assured you the boy will lose his license so he will no longer be a danger to others. What do you do?

Our freedom of the press means that each newspaper editor must answer such questions for himself. In a country with a controlled press, the government makes the decision.

The third, and perhaps the most important, element in the search for truth lies in open controversy. It might be said that the best way to find the truth is to allow every newspaper to print its own version of it, however different these may be.

At the 1964 Republican Convention, ex-President Dwight D. Eisenhower castigated the American press for the way it had covered Republican party affairs. A. J. Liebling, one of the most brilliant critics of American newspapers, took the opposite view that most American newspapers were violently partisan toward the Republican party. Neither the Democrats or the Republicans believe that the press is wholly fair to it, or completely honest in its reporting. As long as this situation exists, we can be sure that our right to know is being protected. If our papers ever please any one partisan group completely, we can be sure that we are getting only part of the news.

Until human beings become perfect, no one person will ever be entirely right about anything, and there will always be two sides to every issue. A controversial press, made up of many newspapers disagreeing with each other, supplies us with enough segments of the truth and variations on it to allow us to make intelligent decisions. No one paper will answer all of our questions satisfactorily, but together they give us the information we need to find our own answers.

Our controversial press tells us both the good and the bad about ourselves and our country. It tells us that our expansive highway programs make driving safer and raise our standard of living, and that they also cost the taxpayer a lot of money and often encroach on private property and destroy natural beauty. It tells us that our federal government should give more financial aid to schools in depressed areas, and also that this may lead to the danger of federal control over education. It tells us that our President is the most important individual in the free world, but it also reports every mistake he makes and prints pictures of him that show him in an unflattering view. It fights crime by publicizing the work of our law enforcement officers, and it embarrasses us by printing our names when we get a traffic ticket. As long as it continues to be controversial, our freedoms are probably safer than at any period in history.

Each controversial news story is balanced between two great aspects of our freedom. The first is the freedom to know, which we believe is the safeguard of our democracy. The second is the freedom to be let alone, which we believe is the safeguard of the individual. Our constitution guarantees our freedom to know, and our libel laws protect our right to be let alone.

In speaking of the American press, we no longer refer only to newspapers. More and more Americans depend regularly on both radio and television for immediate accounts of current news, and most of us read one or more news magazines for detailed and comprehensive accounts of the vital stories of our day. Books may both contain and make news, and some neighborhoods and small towns depend on mimeographed bulletins for local news.

The newspapers of America, however, were the vanguard of the American press, and are still its main voice. Whatever we may think of our newspapers, either individually or collectively, they are as much a part of the American scene as the voting booth, and as vital to our well-being.

2. What Is a Newspaper?

"The people are the voice of God." From the masthead of an old newspaper.

****

Masthead engraved by Paul Revere. Courtesy of American Antiquarian Society.

THE FIRST AMENDMENT to the Bill of Rights contains the first provision ever made by a country to keep its press free. It says, "Congress shall make no law respecting an establishment of religion, or prohibiting the free exercise thereof, or abridging the freedom of speech, or of the press, or of the right of the people peaceably to assemble, and to petition the government for a redress of grievances."

A free press is implemented by newspapers, and newspapers are more complicated and interesting than they may appear at first glance.

A newspaper is a collection of information and entertainment printed on very cheap paper. It may be published daily, weekly, biweekly, or once a month. Most issues of any paper are out of date as soon as the next one is printed.

Yet the contents of newspapers are never out of date, since they are a continuing history of mankind. Libraries keep complete files of many newspapers on microfilm so that they will be permanently available to the public. You can read about most of the important events of the world in history books, but if you want to know what it was like to live through them, the best way to find out is to read the papers that were published at the time.

No two newspapers in America are exactly alike, but each reflects the nature of the place where it is published and the character of those who publish it. Some, like the New York *Times,* are the product of so much knowledge, skill, and concern for our country that they are institutions. At the other end of the scale are numerous papers with little interest in accuracy or public service, but only in making money.

Most large cities have at least one daily newspaper which may be published either in the morning or evening, and often there is both a morning and evening edition. Few towns are so small that they do not have even a weekly newspaper, or a least a section of news in a newspaper printed in a neighboring town.

Anyone who wishes may publish a newspaper. It is not necessary to have taken a certain course of study, or to have passed an examination given by a state or the federal government. Some newspapers are mimeographed pages printed in someone's kitchen, and some that are now large and prosperous began as advertising "throw-aways" which added news to their columns once they had attracted readers.

The newspaper has problems peculiar to itself. It is a private business enterprise that functions as a public institution. While some newspapers are published by private interests and do not necessarily have to make a profit, most of them have to make a profit in order to survive. As public institutions, they are expected to serve the good of the public, but as private business enterprises they must look to their own interests. It has been suggested that since they are necessary for the public welfare the government should help to support them, but the thought of government support carries with it the threat of government supervision, which is repugnant to a free press.

The newspaper has five basic responsibilities: to survive, to provide information, to offer guidance or interpretation of the news, to entertain, and to serve the public.

In order to survive, a newspaper must have sufficient subscribers and advertising to pay all of its expenses and net its owners a suitable return. Roughly speaking, less than one-third of the income of a newspaper comes from subscriptions and newsstand sales, and the rest from advertising. The amount of advertising, however, and the rate per inch, depend on the number of subscribers. Advertisers use newspaper columns to sell their products; they will pay more for space in a well-read newspaper than in one which has few purchasers. It is possible for a newspaper to pretend to have a larger circulation than it does, but it cannot fool its advertisers very long. If advertisements do not bring results, the advertiser can be pretty sure that not many people read them or that they are not influenced by them. For the convenience of advertisers the Audit Bureau of Circulation, a national organization, supplies certified statistics in this field.

Subscribers and newsstand purchasers are gained by the same qualities that sell any manufactured product. Like a new detergent, a newspaper must be up to the minute in its ingredients, it must look attractive, it must serve the need for which it is bought, and it must please the purchaser. Also like a new detergent, a newspaper has many rivals. In a large city, there may or may not be two competing dailies, but there are almost always one or more neighborhood papers which some people find more interesting than the daily. There are also radio and television stations which broadcast news regularly and frequently to anyone who cares to listen, and at no expense to the listener.

The responsibility of providing the news gave newspapers their name. They must gather it, write it, edit it, evaluate it as to the amount of space and emphasis it deserves, and fit it into the news columns. Facilities for gathering news have improved so much that our newspapers now place us at the ringside of important events instead of telling us what happened in the past. European news was several months old before it reached America's first newspapers; now it is reported within a few hours. Every new device for communication is put to use almost as soon as it is invented. A great deal of the mechanical equipment newspapers use was invented specifically for them. Courses are taught in college to help young people train to become newspaper workers and many colleges and universities grant degrees in journalism. Elementary and grade schools teach students to read and understand the news they see printed in newspapers.

Newspapers provide guidance for their readers in many ways. Chief among them are deciding which news is of most importance, and giving a background of information which includes both sides of all issues. There are always a number of things going on at the same time in any locality and no newspaper has time or space to give all of them complete coverage. Its editors must decide whether the local garden show or the presidential primary is of more vital concern to its readers and just how important each one is. This decision is based on other news in the same area as well as on the interests of the readers. Some small town newspapers print very little national and international news since they believe their readers get this from large daily newspapers whose circulation overlaps theirs and from radio and television.

Reporting both sides of every issue is more difficult and just as important. An editor, who may be an opinionated man, may be convinced that his viewpoint about a proposed town ordinance is the correct one and that anyone who disagrees with him is an idiot. Yet he owes it to his readers to dig up the opinions and facts submitted by the opposition and print them in his paper. If he is a good editor, he will make sure that his opinions are restricted to the editorial columns and that they are neither a part of nor allowed to influence the news columns.

Some critics do not approve of the efforts of newspapers to entertain their readers. They say that too much valuable space is given to movie columns, crossword puzzles, comic strips, and other features which have nothing to do with news. These may build circulation and advertising, they say, but they tend to cheapen a newspaper.

This must be considered a matter of opinion. Grocery stores sell many items on which they make almost no profit in order to get customers into the store where they will buy other things. Newspapers must please their readers, or they will have no readers. Constant studies are made of what people read most in newspapers, and few unpopular features survive. Newspapers will continue to entertain their readers to the best of their ability as long as that is what their readers wish.

Newspapers serve the public by performing all of their functions well, and also by acting as a public conscience. They dig up stories affecting the public welfare and publicize injustice. They act as a constant goad to elected and appointed officials by keeping their readers informed about government, and they assist worthy causes by promoting them in news stories and pictures.

Good newspapers are constantly crusading for things they believe are worthwhile. The Charlotte (N.C.) *Observer* ran a series entitled "Our Neglected Children," which dealt with mental health problems of North Carolina children. The New York *Times* is famous for its "Hundred Neediest Cases" campaign which it runs each year to encourage donations to the underprivileged in the city. The York (Pa.) *Dispatch,* beginning on November 24, 1959, and ending on March 2, 1960, devoted 44 tons of newsprint and 4,500 overtime hours to a campaign to print the county's reassessment figures, which covered approximately 80,000 separate parcels of real estate in the 15 city wards, 36 boroughs, and 35 townships, as a public service.

Every local, regional, and national organization working for the public welfare expects and gets substantial support in the form of publicity in newspapers. Churches, schools, libraries, government agencies, and clubs depend on news stories to promote their activities.

A newspaper has five main divisions: editorial, mechanical, business, promotion, and administrative.

The editorial department gathers, writes, edits, and illustrates the news and supplies the editorials for the newspaper. The business office manages the circulation and advertising departments and takes care of accounting, pay roll, and records. The promotion department toots the paper's own horn by running contests, publicizing the paper's value to the community and its readers, and working in every way to promote the paper. The mechanical department handles the physical production of the newspaper. News and advertising copy is set into type, pictures and illustrations are made into cuts, and everything is assembled in page-size steel chases. Plates are cast from these chases, which are then ready for the presses. The administrative department is made up of the owner and executives whose job it is to coordinate the various operations of the newspaper and establish policies.

All of this is behind the printed sheets which about 95 per cent of the people in America buy regularly for a few cents, spend about eighteen minutes reading, and then discard.

3.

What Is
in a Newspaper?

"A typical metropolitan daily newspaper contains about 100,000 words of reading matter." From *A Nose for News is not Enough*, published by The Bell Telephone System.

****

Lebanon, N. H. *Valley News* Wins Ayer Cup in 1964 for excellence of typography, make-up and printing.

HOW MANY OF US REALLY KNOW

what is in a newspaper?

Most of us would say news, editorials, pictures, sports, and the comic strips—and perhaps our favorite columnists. We read selectively so that few of us realize the vast number of things that most newspapers contain every day. (Some years ago a survey was taken to see how many people knew the number of columns of print on a newspaper page. The number who knew was surprisingly small!)

Newspapers contain national and international news, state news, and community news. There is regular news in a dozen different categories: births, deaths, local recreation programs, church services, traffic courts, fire calls, hospital listings, library programs, police news, announcements of coming events, market bulletins, stock market reports, the U.S. Treasury balance, weather news (which includes phases of the moon, temperature and barometer readings, a comparison of the current weather to that of a year before, and in certain localities the hours of low and high tides), and probably different items in different communities.

There are special pages or sections devoted to specific groups of readers—the women's pages, the sports pages, sometimes a page for children.

The editorial page carries editorials written by the editor or a members of his staff (or purchased from a syndicate), nationally syndicated columns of news and opinion, and often columns about local affairs. This is the page of opinion; the editor and his staff and the columnists say what they think about what is going on. Letters to the editor are found here, telling what the readers think about what is going on, and what they think of the news and opinions of the newspaper.

Editorials can make enemies for papers but they can build a reputation for honesty and integrity if they are thoughtful, intelligent, and fair-minded. William Allen White, while the editor of a small newspaper in Kansas, gained a nationwide reputation for the excellence of his editorials on local and national affairs.

Nationally syndicated columns bring news and opinions of experts in various fields to even the smallest towns. Columnists, mostly political, are as varied in their viewpoints as the many papers in which they appear. It is the custom of many papers to use the columns of those who agree with them politically, while others regularly use columns which present various viewpoints about the same problems and situations.

Letters to the editor are often printed on the editorial page, though sometimes there are enough of them to fill a page of their own. It has often been said that a newspaper can be judged by the number and quality of its letters to the editor because they indicate how much influence the paper has on its readers, and the quality of the readers themselves. Very few papers print all of the letters they receive, for a number of reasons. Newspapers receive many letters from cranks whose outpourings are sometimes not intelligible and often of little interest to anyone other than the writer. They also receive letters containing statements which would make the paper, as well as the writer, open to a libel suit. A good newspaper takes great pains to print letters from those whose viewpoints oppose its own and letters criticizing its policies and contents. The citizen who wishes to make his influence felt will make use of this opportunity to work for what he believes is right.

Newspapers contain material that may be considered either news or entertainment: theatrical reviews, book reviews, television and radio programs. There are comic strips and horoscopes, crossword puzzles and cartoons. There are even what are known as "fillers": brief items, set in odd spots to fill space, give such facts as "The Gulf Stream flows faster in summer than in winter," or "A London, England, window cleaner was fined $14 (sic) for biting the nose of a man who pushed past him in a bus line."

Scattered throughout the paper are advertisements, and to many readers they are almost as important as the news. They tell of sales and bargains and what can be bought where. They announce lost dogs and found bracelets, workers available, and help wanted. The advertisements in some papers are so attractive they almost over-shadow the news, and certainly they perform a public service to the householder who purchases for the family. Reputable newspapers are careful about the advertisements they print and the improve-ment in this area has been marked in the last hundred years. During the Civil War it was common to see miraculous patent drugs advertised on the front pages of otherwise respectable papers and many readers thought them as much to be believed as the news stories and editorials.

The comic strips in American newspapers are popular around the world, as well as here. Children in other countries know some of our favorite cartoon characters as well as we do, and some for-eign peoples believe that they are a true picture of American life.

Generally speaking, everything that appears in the columns of newspapers is of interest to a certain number of readers or it would not be there. One exception may be a newspaper with no competi-tion which is sure to get enough advertising money to support it.

Under these circumstances, some such papers fill their pages with whatever material requires the least effort and make no serious effort to serve the community.

The contents of a good newspaper are the result of serious thought and hard work by the editorial and advertising staff. They include both what will interest the reader, and what is for the public welfare.

Such a paper gives us a good picture of what our life is like: how we live, what we do, the things we think about, the motives and issues that concern us. The good newspaper and the good reader are involved in the serious business of trying to understand man and the universe in which he lives.

4.

What Is News?

"All the news that's fit to print"—Motto of the New York *Times*,
first printed October 25, 1896.

❊❊❊

WHAT IS NEWS? It is the honest and un-biased and complete account of events of interest and concern to the public.

A typical metropolitan daily may receive approximately 8 million words of copy each day from its staff, wire services, feature syndi-cates, correspondents and special writers. Of this, only about 100,-000 can be used in the paper.

Local stories are gathered by staff reporters and correspondents. Each reporter is responsible for certain types of news and some have what are called "beats." One may cover the city offices, another the police court and state police, someone else the society news. Correspondents from neighborhood areas and surrounding towns write or telephone news from their localities.

A reporter on his beat will make notes of various stories he en-counters, then return to the office and write them. On a larger paper, or during an emergency when time is precious, he may phone them in to the "desk" where a rewrite man will take them.

Other people also telephone in stories or suggestions for stories. No newspaper has enough reporters to cover every spot where news may break, nor can it possibly keep up with all of the activities in any town. Members of the public and town officials frequently no-tify a paper when an important issue is coming up in a town meeting, when a deer has wandered into a suburban neighborhood, or when a certain couple is planning to celebrate a golden wedding anniversary.

Public relations and publicity people for all sorts of individuals and organizations regularly send stories to newspapers. Some of these stories are legitimate news, and some are merely designed to keep clients in the spotlight of public attention.

Foreign and out-of-state news stories often carry a set of initials in the dateline which indicates that they were supplied by one of the wire services. AP means Associated Press. UPI means United Press International. Such a story from New York, for instance, was covered by a wire service staff member at the spot where it occurred and phoned in to the New York office. It was handled by a rewrite man, then edited and teletyped to subscribing New York bureaus and to regional bureau offices throughout the country. At each regional office it was again edited before being teletyped to subscribing newspapers in the area. This editing is done to fit the needs of out-of-town papers which will not want as long a story as those near the area where the event happened. At the local paper, a city editor or news editor evaluated the story and decided where it was to be used in his paper. He then passed it to the copy desk where it was again refined, pared to a specific length, and headlined. It was scrutinized by an editorial board before being sent to the composing room. A newspaper which subscribes to a wire service may edit stories to fit its needs but may not change the content or slant them without removing the wire service identification.

All news stories, once written, are edited and designated for particular spots in the paper. Their length, their position and whether or not news photos accompany them will depend on their importance compared to other news in the same issue.

There is a well-known truism about news that defines it as something out of the ordinary. It says that if a dog bites a man it is not news, but that if a man bites a dog, it *is* news. Anyone who reads the average newspaper will realize that this hardly applies to a large per cent of what is presented to him as news. Much space in all newspapers is devoted to ordinary, expected, and not particularly surprising events:

The Elks have a picnic, the PTA holds a reception for new members, the League of Women Voters offers transportation to the polls, the Little League wins a game, ten speeders are fined in police court—these stories, multiplied a thousand-fold, appear daily in newspapers all across America.

Seemingly even less important and exciting than these are what are called "meet-the-train" items. "Mr. and Mrs. Joseph Smith were dinner guests at the home of Mr. and Mrs. Sam Brown on Thursday, March 19." "Miss Jane Brown has returned home from Chatham College, where she has just completed her junior year." Newspapers value these stories more than you might suppose because they are so important to those whose names are mentioned.

The "big" stories, the hurricane that demolishes a town, the child lost in the woods, the bank robbery, the escaped criminal, do not happen so often, and may well be called "man bites dog" stories.

The type of story that is hardest to get and offers the most potential danger to a paper is the one kept hidden from the public. The good reporter and the good editor are never content with routine news and regular "handouts" from official sources, but are always on the alert for what is not easy to see.

A city plans a huge new park in a residential area. It is much needed to provide recreation facilities for large numbers of children. On the other hand, who now owns the land where it will be located, and when did they buy it? (Did the plans leak from certain city officials so that relatives and friends could buy the land at a low price, to resell later at a profit?) How much will be paid for the land, and who decides on its value? How are the contracts for the necessary work to be awarded? Who has written the specifications for construction and will everything be of the best quality? The alert paper seeking this information will have no difficulty if all city officials are honest, but a crooked administration will resent a public scrutiny of its affairs. The paper that battles dishonest public officials is asking for trouble, but many a good paper has brought about great social reforms by doing just that.

News in American newspapers is supposed to be honest, accurate, concise, and easy to understand. It should not be written to serve any special interests, groups, or individuals. Most reporters and editors pride themselves on living up to these standards. It is much more difficult than it might seem to be sure that this is always done.

News which gives a one-sided impression is "slanted." A reporter or editor can, consciously or unconsciously, slant news in many different ways.

The selection of which stories to print may slant the news. Some Southern newspapers have carried almost no news about racial difficulties in their areas, which may have given the impression that such things did not exist there. Some Northern newspapers have ignored stories of racial difficulties in the North, but headlined those in the South, which may have given the impression that it was a purely regional problem. During a presidential campaign, partisan Republican papers may print countless stories about the huge crowds attending speeches made by the Republican candidate and hardly mention the same sort of crowds present to hear the Democratic candidate. Partisan Democratic papers may run stories showing the popularity of their candidate, and select those which show a lack of popularity on the part of his opponent.

When done deliberately, this sort of slanting defeats the purpose of giving the public a clear and balanced picture of current events. It is often done, in a minor way, with no such intention. The editor who is an avid sports fan is apt to have a larger sports section than the one who is uninterested in sports but deeply involved in politics. The reporter who is fascinated by the business growth of the city will see more stories there than in its schools.

Responsible editors are aware that they often "create" news by selecting it for their columns. There are dozens of different departments in any state government, and news is apt to be in the making in all of them most of the time. The highway department is planning new roads, the department of employment is devising new tests for prospective employees, the treasurer has a report on the state's financial condition, the state promotion department is running a contest to choose a state flower, the state police department is reorganizing, the governor is making a speech, the welfare department reports an unusually heavy case load, the state park authority wants to create a new park in land reclaimed by a flood control project. Most of these matters are routine and might ordinarily be handled by routine news treatment.

Suppose that the newspaper editor decides that the matter of reclaimed land is of the utmost importance to the state, either because he thinks it should be a park or because he thinks it should be left untouched and used for a wild life refuge. He can put a good reporter on the story, set him to work digging up background and similar situations in other states, and run a series of front page stories which treat the matter as if it were the only really vital thing going on in the state. He could do the same with any one of the listed stories and give it importance at the expense of other news.

The attempt to make a paper interesting and exciting can slant news. Some newspapers fill their columns with stories of crime, tragedy, and corruption in order to attract readers; this makes it seem that these are the only noteworthy things happening. Other papers, wishing to help their communities by keeping everyone happy, err on the other side and rarely print anything unpleasant.

The position of a particular news story on the page and the page on which it appears, the number of words used for it, whether or not it is illustrated, and the way in which it is headlined can slant news.

Remember our fictitious governor who was involved in a traffic accident? Let us assume that it was snowing, that he was driving down a hill where children were sliding on the sidewalk, and that his car went out of control, narrowly missed another one, and crashed into a tree. He was examined by a doctor but was found to be uninjured. Think of the different headlines that could be written for such a story: "Governor Escapes Death in Accident," "Governor to Face Court Charges in Accident," "Children Uninjured by Governor's Accident, Is Claim"—and so on.

News may be slanted by lack of time and manpower to pursue it thoroughly. A newspaper may get a tip that a Mr. Peter Smith has been victimized by the state highway department. A reporter is sent to investigate the incident.

He finds Mr. Smith, aged 79, living near a new highway but unable to have a driveway built between it and his house. He had previously lived at another location, but his land was confiscated by the highway department to make room for the new highway. Being too poor to hire a lawyer, he had taken the price offered for his land by the state. A neighbor had interceded with the state on his behalf and helped him buy back his original home, which had then been moved to its present spot. Once settled, he had planted a garden, bought a cow, built a henhouse, and *then* had found that the state would not allow him to build the necessary driveway. His only access to the outside world is a path a quarter of a mile long which leads to a secondary road. He cannot afford to turn this into a proper driveway because the only money he has is the amount the state paid him for his former property.

The reporter finds this a heart-rending story and returns to his office to write it. His editor looks it over carefully. It is interesting, the public should know about it if it is a typical incident, and it is true in the sense that it is reported exactly as Mr. Smith told it. If it turns out not to be the complete truth, the paper is not in danger of a libel suit, because the state cannot bring such a suit. (In our country, the government *is* the people, and we cannot sue ourselves. If a story accuses a specific government official of something that may harm his reputation, he can bring suit as an individual on the basis of personal injury.)

The editor suggests that the reporter telephone the proper state official and get the state's side of the story. The reporter makes the call and is connected with a man who has a desk full of important work and no inclination to talk. The official says he is sick and tired of hearing about Mr. Smith and of the way newspaper reporters distort facts. Here is another angle to the story. "State official angered by questions, has no sympathy for Mr. Smith, and accuses newspapers of distorting the truth." It becomes more colorful by the minute.

A good reporter does not stop there. He should insist on his right to know the facts and should explain that the story is going to be printed and he would like to make it as accurate as possible. (Most state officials and others in public life realize it is always better to talk to the press than to refuse to, no matter what they may happen to think of the individual reporter or newspaper concerned.)

A subsequent interview will present new facts. The state is involved in a large-scale operation of highway construction, and the property of Mr. Smith is one of many it has purchased. All such property has been evaluated by professional appraisers to determine its true value. Mr. Smith was informed, by letter, that he could buy back his original home at a modest price, as were all uprooted home owners. He was further advised, again by letter, that the property to which he had his house moved would not be allowed access to the new highway. Most new highways, such as this one, have limited side access in order to prevent dangerous cross traffic.

The state official might eventually become more friendly with the reporter and advise him that Mr. Smith is a well-known crank who has caused endless trouble. He may suggest that it would be wise to drop the whole story, since it is obviously not a case of right or wrong, but of a man who can get along with no one.

This changes the story entirely, and the reporter and the paper have now spent considerable time on it—time which would otherwise have gone to other stories. Is this the end?

Not yet. The reporter should check the official records and interview other state officials and those whose property has been purchased for the same highway. Out of all this time and effort may come a story that uncovers wrongdoing on the part of the state, or a story that is hardly worth writing and printing. Few newspapers have the facilities for following up every suggested story to this extent. *A story that is incomplete may be slanted because it omits some of the facts.*

Some stories may be both true and important, but misleading. Some years ago the late Senator Joseph McCarthy undertook a crusade to rid the government, schools, and churches of people whom he considered sympathetic to Communism. Speaking in the Senate (where his senatorial immunity made him safe from libel suits), he began to name people whom he said were Communists, Communist sympathizers, or "soft on Communism." Many of them were prominent people whose names were as newsworthy as the senator's.

It is news when any government official makes such statements. Many thoughtful editors did not believe the charges were true but they could not ignore their news value nor express their opinions in the news stories themselves. In order to handle the matter in what they considered the proper perspective, they printed their opinions on the editorial page, made a consistent effort to follow up on all of the accusations and give their readers the facts. Some published interviews with those accused giving their background and stature and with people who opposed Senator McCarthy's project.

To return to our original definition, news is an honest, unbiased, and complete account of events of interest or concern to the public. Professor George H. Morris of Florida Southern University, who was a newspaperman for many years before he became a teacher, characterizes news as "history in a hurry." He says "Read several papers, day after day, and eventually the truth will emerge."

No newspaper, because of the limitations of time and space, can print all of the facts that make the news in any one issue. No reader can understand what is happening by scanning any one issue of any one paper.

It is difficult for even the best newspaper to do a good job of gathering and writing the news. The good reader will evaluate it by reading carefully day after day and comparing the way identical stories are covered in papers with different viewpoints.

5. What Is a Newsman?

"A good newspaperman has no friends."

ERWIN CANHAM

JAMES RESTON
The New York Times

Arnold Newman

WILLIAM L. SHIRER

EDWARD R. MURROW

A REPORTER is one who gathers and writes news; an editor is one who evaluates, edits, and positions it in the paper. Many editors were once reporters, and a reporter must have a good understanding of the editorial requirements of his paper to do a good job. Both are newsmen—a term not applied to members of the business, promotion, or administrative departments.

All newsmen are not as glamorous, handsome, and exciting as their fictional and television counterparts, but the picture is not an entirely false one. There is an excitement and satisfaction connected with newspaper work that few other fields can match. Those who succeed in it have certain characteristics and abilities not required in other professions. (To succeed in newspaper work does not necessarily mean to become rich and famous but to do a good job of reporting the truth.)

One of the qualities which makes news work so exciting is the feeling of "being on top of the news." Each of us has had the satisfaction of being the first in a group to learn a special bit of news, and this is the normal state of affairs with a newsman. He knows which congressman is going to run for senator, how wide the main street is going to be, which member of the city council is planning to resign, and why the mayor wants elm trees instead of oaks in the new city park. He is a friend of those in high places, and of those in low. He is equally at home at a Rotary Club luncheon and at a reception for the governor of the state. He understands the local educational system and the workings of the police court. He expects to be, and usually is, welcome in places where members of the public are not invited—at fires, at the scene of accidents, near the speaker's table at banquets, at any place where calamities occur, at official meetings, and any place a news story may break.

The requirements for being a good newsman may not be as rigorous as they have been in the past, but they often seem formidable. He must know enough about almost anything that can happen to be able to make sense of any event that occurs. A man who had never seen a baseball game would not understand his first one well enough to know what was going on. The reporter sent to cover an accident should know something about cars, about how to drive, about road conditions, traffic laws, and previous similar accidents, to understand this one clearly. He needs to know what his paper will require for a story—the names and ages of those involved, the names, makes, years, and owners' names of the car or cars, the time of day, the location, the weather, road, and traffic conditions which contributed to the accident, the charge to be brought by the investigating police, the condition of possible victims, the time of day or night it occurred, and the probable outcome. He needs to know what he may report and what he may not. Although he may be quite sure that one of the drivers was drunk and had been driving recklessly, he may not say so until it is an official charge made by the police. Most preliminary newspaper accounts of accidents say that a driver "lost control of his car" or that the car "went out of control" without giving any cause.

Frequently the reporter who gathers material for a story also carries his own camera and takes pictures to go with it. This is the day of photo-journalism.

After he has done all of these things he must return to the office and write a clear, accurate and understandable story of exactly what happened, tailored to a length set by his editor.

The reporter must be able to work under extreme pressure of time and excitement without losing his ability to see clearly, understand quickly, and write well. He must know where to go for the information he requires, and how to get it from people who may not necessarily want to give it.

A good newsman, working for a good newspaper, takes great pride in being on the side of the truth against everything else. When a story breaks, his only concern is to get as much of the truth as accurately as possible, regardless of whose feelings may be hurt, whose prestige may be damaged, whose status may be raised, or who may write an indignant letter to the paper. A grocery-store clerk is not expected to quarrel with a customer, an insurance salesman does not wish to antagonize a client, a businessman does not want to quarrel openly with a rival. None of these considerations is supposed to deter a newsman in search of the truth. If the governor of the state is involved in a scandal, if the newsman's best friend is accused of stealing from his employer, if a banker absconds with funds, this is news—and the news is more important than business or personal considerations.

This is the reason for the saying, "A good newspaperman has no friends," to which is often added "and no enemies."

In the first part of this century, Joseph Pulitzer was searching for an editor for his newspaper, the New York *World*. He sent a telegram to a friend who had recommended Frank I. Cobb of the Detroit *Free Press,* defining what he considered necessary qualities for the position. In language that now seems old fashioned, it said, "What has Cobb read in American history? . . . what works on the Constitution and Constitutional Law? Has he read Buckle's *History of Civilization?* . . . What about the state of his health? How tall is he? Is his voice harsh or agreeable? . . . Take him out to dinner and note his table manners. Is his disposition cheerful?

Sound out his ambitions; whether satisfied, or looking to a larger field . . . describe minutely his appearance, color of eyes, shape of forehead, mannerisms, how he dresses. Search his brain for everything there is in it."

The color of a man's eyes and the shape of his forehead would not seem to have much to do with his ability as an editor and probably no prospective employer would make an issue of them today. However, coupled with his table manners, his disposition, his mannerisms, his voice, and his way of dressing, they all add up to personality and appearance, which are still very important. A newspaperman does not need to win a charm contest, but he should be poised, presentable, and worthy of acceptance in any circle where his work may take him.

The emphasis on background knowledge, even in such fields as constitutional law, is perhaps even more important today. Nobel prize-winner Polykarp Kusch, speaking at Columbia University during the 50th anniversary of the School of Journalism, said, "The most important challenge to journalism may be to devise a way to give all men a sense of the continuity of the human experience."

One of the problems much debated in political affairs is that of states' rights versus federal rights. It is sometimes to the interest of a particular politician to present the issue as if the federal government were an ogre intent on devouring a weak and defenseless state—or for another politician to insist that a certain state government is acting in defiance of constitutional law. Whatever truth is in either charge can be known only if the newsman covering the story has a background knowledge of how our Founding Fathers agreed upon the respective rights of federal and state governments, how they have been interpreted in various court decisions since, and what the current status is. He can only understand the contemporary scene if he knows how it was brought about and the reasons for it.

J. R. Wiggins, Executive Editor of the Washington *Post,* said that the obligations assumed by the press in recent years have grown much more rapidly than the ability of the press to handle them, which may make the coverage of news lopsided. Newspapers are not satisfied to report isolated news stories as they occur, according to Mr. Wiggins, but attempt to give a solid background which clarifies them. A reporter in Washington, D.C., whose job it is to cover the various government bureaus, should know something about the tax structure of our country, the problems of the farmer, the government printing office, national defense, education, public relief, highways, the labor situation, and several hundred other areas. He should also have or acquire the same sort of background on the office-holders he will meet and interview and the offices they hold. The more the reporter knows, the better the job he can do.

Ralph McGill, Pulitzer prize-winner and editor of the Atlanta *Constitution,* says, "You can't really hope to be much of a writer, it seems to me, unless you like to read. It takes a person who is fundamentally intelligent and fundamentally curious to do a lot of reading, and curiosity is, to me, one of the most important traits a journalist can have. In many ways, curiosity is the most important quality of all. If you aren't curious, I don't see how you can hope to write at all."

What is curiosity? It is a deep and active interest in everything that happens, and the reason behind it. Most news stories are the result of a reporter asking questions, and the better the questions, the better the story. A reporter without an adequate background of knowledge will not know what questions to ask; a reporter without curiosity will not be aggressive enough to ask questions at all. He will accept whatever is told him, and thus miss the story he should be getting.

James Reston, formerly chief Washington correspondent of the New York *Times* and winner of two Pulitzer prizes, says good newsmen have another quality—"Vitality, drive, aliveness, call it what you will." He was not speaking just of physical energy but of a mental trait. Such a person finds the world and the people in it exciting, and he feels involved in everything that happens. A political upset in Europe, new lighting fixtures in the elementary school, a town ordinance about curbing dogs, and a blight that is killing maple trees—all are of concern to him. His reporting will be more alive, and this vitality will be conveyed to his readers.

Another characteristic of the good newsman is described by Douglass Cater, editor of *The Reporter*. In his book, *The Fourth Branch of Our Government*, Mr. Cater says it is the belief of the good newsman that "progress comes through controversy. . . . He believes in the purifying powers of publicity. He is the sworn enemy of secrecy."

This is a trait without which no controversial news story would ever be written, and which gets many newsmen into trouble.

A reporter covering the police court learns that a certain policeman is going to be fired. He takes this information to the chief of police, who asks him to kill the story. The erring policeman has been found guilty of taking bribes from a gambler and has admitted his guilt. He is not going to be fired, but has resigned. The matter is settled, and airing it publicly will damage the public image of the police force and create suspicion of all police in the minds of the citizens. It may even be suggested that the police department expects cooperation from the reporter in return for the cooperation it gives him.

Similar situations are faced over and over by newsmen in the course of their work. Individuals among them have had great pressures brought to bear to keep them from getting stories, they have been threatened with loss of their jobs, foreclosure of their mortgages, stoppage of their news sources, and even personal injury. To combat this sort of influence, the good newsman needs courage and a deep sense of integrity. When his integrity tells him the public welfare is concerned, his courage must be great enough to make him persevere.

Since writing is the basic skill of the newsman, he must be able to select and handle words well. The day of long-winded journalism is past, and a brief but brilliant news story is much more difficult to write than a wordy one. A good newsman has an extensive vocabulary and uses words for their exact, rather than their approximate, meaning.

A good newsman, then, should be at home in the world in which he lives, he should have knowledge, curiosity, vitality, a sense of controversy, courage, integrity, and a way with words. Perhaps we should say of him, "He has no friends—but the truth."

6. What Is Libel?

"I can take that LaGuardia, too, any time, because he is a bull-dozing four-flusher and he will tin-can it and back away, squealing like a pig under a gate if you carry it right to him and never let go." Westbrook Pegler, a sample from one of his columns in the New York *World Telegram*.

****

The New York Times

WESTBROOK PEGLER rose to national fame through his vigorous and outspoken columns. After years of success, he lost a widely publicized libel suit brought against him by another newsman, Quentin Reynolds. Mr. Reynolds was awarded one of the largest sums ever granted by a court in a libel suit. The quotation opposite is Mr. Pegler's comment about the then mayor of New York.

William A. DeFord, attorney-at-law, said, "Most libel suits are risked, not intentionally, but through pure carelessness, and for this reason can and should be avoided. It would be extremely careless of a newspaper to make a charge which it could not substantiate." The matter is actually much more complicated than that.

All news stories are bounded by two concepts of our rights as citizens and as individuals. The first is our "right to know," which says that our government belongs to us, that the law and order of the country are our responsibility, our public officials are people we have chosen to work for us, and all of this is our business. The other concept is the "right to be let alone," which says that our private lives are our own business, that we cannot be condemned, persecuted, or humiliated because of our beliefs, our differences from others, or our way of doing things.

Libel laws, though they differ in various states, are designed to protect our right to be let alone. In general terms, a libel is anything printed or written which tends to humiliate, embarrass, harm, or hold up to ridicule the person about whom it is written. It is obviously impossible to publish a newspaper which serves the public and *not* libel someone at some time or other. The essence of libel is *exposure,* and everything printed in a newspaper is exposed to the world.

45

It is generally believed that "the truth is a defense against libel," but this is only partly true. A newspaper that can prove that what it has printed is true may or may not be safe from a libel suit. It depends on what it printed, and why—the motive behind the publication of the story.

A newspaper may print a story it cannot prove which indicates malfeasance on the part of a public official and pay no penalty at all. It may publish a fully documented and completely accurate story proving that a present bank president is a former criminal who was convicted of robbery and served time in jail, and find itself faced with a huge libel suit. The *reason* for the story has as much legal importance as the story itself. The newspaper that can prove that its purpose is the public welfare is on fairly safe ground; the paper whose only motive is malice is in trouble. (In the case of the banker, he has paid the penalty for his misdeed, and will contend legally that he cannot be forced to pay it again.)

It should also be understood that not everyone who is libeled by a newspaper brings suit, that not every libel suit is won by the plaintiff, and that sometimes the damages awarded are so small they do little harm to the paper.

An actual libel is considered to be as damaging to the person libeled as a physical assault, but it is not nearly as clear-cut. If John Jones knocks Bill Smith to the ground and kicks him, the matter is fairly obvious. Bill Smith has suffered damage which can be assessed by a physician, but a court must decide how much damage a supposed libel has done.

The ways in which a newspaper may libel someone are countless. Suppose that John Jones is editor of the town newspaper and Joe Smith is chief of police. A relative of Smith's tells Editor Jones that the police chief has been accepting bribes from a nightclub which runs illegal gambling tables. The relative refuses to be quoted, but there is no doubt that his story is true.

Editor Jones cannot report the story to the police, since the head of the police is involved. He has no actual evidence to take to any law enforcement agency, and he feels that the matter should be made public at once. There are two courses of action open to him.

Lacking the support of the police, he can begin work to prove that the story is true. This would require many hours of searching for evidence and of trying to find witnesses who would talk. News of his activities would soon reach the police chief, who would take immediate steps to undermine them.

His second course is to expose the story in his newspaper. There are many ways in which he can do this:

publish it on the front page, as a news story, without naming the person who gave him his information.

publish it as a news story, and name the person who gave him his information.

publish a news story which does not name Joe Smith, but refers to "a highly placed law enforcement officer."

print a story which says there is rumor that the police chief has been protecting gambling interests in the town.

print a story deploring the terrible rumor that the police chief has been protecting gambling interests in the town.

print an editorial expressing his opinion that the police chief has been accepting bribes.

print a "Letter to the Editor" signed by a prominent citizen, making the charge against Smith.

print a nationally syndicated column written by a prominent

Washington correspondent, which lists his town as one of a number in which police and gambling interests are combined.

print a cartoon which shows a character named Smith playing cards with a gambler.

print a mythical story in which an imaginary character named Psmith protects the villains whom he is supposed to be fighting.

print an advertisement, written and paid for by a group of local merchants who sign their names, which makes the charge against Smith.

In each case he has used the power of the press to reveal an unsavory situation, and in each of them he has made himself liable to a libel suit. (In the case of the "Letter to the Editor" and of the syndicated column and of the advertisement, he can be sued for libel because he "exposed" it in his paper.)

If Jones is lucky, his efforts may arouse public and official opinion so that something is done about the erring police chief. If he is unlucky, he may lose a libel suit.

There are, however, certain types of comments and criticisms which newspapers are legally entitled to make. They are called "fair comment."

The American novelist, James Fenimore Cooper, helped establish this principle. He owned a point of land jutting into a lake which the public had used freely for a number of years. When he decided to stop this practice and post the land with "No Trespassing" signs, it was deeply resented.

Comments about his action appeared in the press, and reviews of his books began to be filled with criticisms of him as a person. Mr. Cooper, in a long series of suits against the papers which printed such reviews, contended that a book review could properly say what it pleased about the *book* in question, but should not contain personal comments about its author.

These suits helped to settle the matter of "fair comment." Anyone who creates anything for public consideration, performs in public, or leads a public life, may expect free comment on that part of his creation, performance, or existence which is public. Beyond this fair comment may not go.

In March 1964 a Supreme Court ruling established a new concept of libel and gave newspapers greater freedom than they had enjoyed before:

On March 29, 1960, a full-page ad had been published in the York *Times,* paid for by friends of integration leader Dr. Martin Luther King, Jr., which solicited funds for his defense against charges of state income tax evasion. In its content, the ad charged that armed police in Montgomery, Alabama, had helped subdue a student civil rights protest, and had also locked students out of the dining hall to starve them into submission. The ad further charged "Southern violators" with bombing Dr. King's home and arresting him seven times.

Five public officials in Alabama brought suit for damages against the *Times,* although none of them had been named in the ad. The *Times* admitted that there were inaccuracies in the ad. Juries in Alabama decided that it was libelous and awarded damages of $500,000.

The *Times* appealed its case to the Supreme Court and the former verdict was repealed. More than that, it cast doubts on the constitutionality of libel laws in Alabama and in many other states.

The Supreme Court decision of March 1964 emphasized a profound national commitment to the principle that debate on public issues "should be uninhibited, robust, and wide open, and . . . it may well include vehement, caustic, and sometimes unpleasantly sharp attacks on government and public officials." On the matter of the inaccuracies in the ad, Justice William J. Brennan, speaking for the court, said, "We consider that the proof presented to show actual malice lacks the convincing clarity which the constitutional standard demands."

Time, commenting on the verdict, said, "The public conduct of public officials, the court ruled, is henceforth fair game, even if the criticism is misguided, unwarranted, undeserved or untrue. If the injured party expects to collect any damages, he will have to prove that the criticism was deliberately or recklessly false—in short, that malice was involved."

Our libel laws are designed to protect our right to be let alone, and the legal interpretation of them is designed to protect the freedom of the press. Both are necessary to a democracy.

7. What Is Freedom of the Press?

"The Liberty of the Press, like Civil Liberty, is talked of by many and understood but by few." From *The Independent Reflector of* August 30, 1753.

****

Andrew Hamilton, Defender of Peter Zenger.

WE BELIEVE THAT WE HAVE FREEDOM
of the press in America, and yet the matter is still being discussed
and argued; this quotation from *The Independent Reflector* is as
true today as it was when written.

In 1671 Governor Berkeley of Virginia said, "I thank God we
have no free schools or printing: and I hope that we shall not have
them these hundred years. For learning has brought disobedience
and heresy and sects into the world: and printing has divulged
them and libels against the government. God keep us from both."

Nineteen years later, on Thursday, September 25, 1690, America's first newspaper was printed on a hand press in a wooden shack
on a narrow street in Boston. The date was seventy years after the
landing of the Pilgrims and almost two hundred years after the
discovery of America by Columbus.

This newspaper, *Publick Occurrences,* was four sheets about the
size of a piece of typing paper, with only three of them printed.
Readers were invited to write their own news on the blank page
before passing their copy along. (Only a few copies of any of the
early papers were printed, and it was assumed that many people
would read each copy. They were often posted in such places as
coffee houses to make them more available to the public.)

The general tone of the little paper was warm and gossipy and to
us it would seem quite harmless. Yet two of the stories it contained
produced such consternation, as well as the consternation aroused
by the very appearance of a newspaper at all, that it was immediately suppressed. The first issue was the only one.

One of these stories was about an attack on the French in Canada which it was said certain groups of Indians had urged and had
agreed to assist. When the expedition was ready to leave, these

same Indians said they could not go because of smallpox. The concluding paragraph read, "Where lay the bottom of these mis-carriages is variously conjectured, if people further West than Albany have been tampering with the Indians, to desert the business of Canada, we hope time will discover it. And if the Almighty God will have Canada to be subdued without the assistances of these miserable Savages, in whom we have too much confided, we shall be glad that there will be no sacrifice offered up to the Devil, upon this occasion, God alone will have all the glory."

The other story which disturbed the authorities was brief. "*France* is in much trouble (and fear not only with us but also with his Son, who has revolted against him lately, and has great reason) if reports be true."

It is necessary to read between the lines to understand why these items should have seemed so terrible to the authorities of colonial Boston. The first made a charge of corruption and the second hinted at a scandal in the French court. These are exactly the sort of libels against the government that Governor Berkeley said printing divulged.

We must step back into history to understand why comments about government were considered libel. English law, which governed the colonies, was designed to protect the existing order of society. Government was in the hands of a group of people, beginning with the king and descending through his officials, who upheld and maintained its regulations. The ordinary citizen was not thought capable of understanding how countries should be run, and certainly not of commenting on the government or criticizing it. The only legal newspapers were those licensed by the state, and only those which could be expected to print what was safe for ordinary people to know were given licenses. Any free and open comment about laws, individual officials, or the government itself might well tend to destroy the respect of the people for the government, and therefore it was not permitted.

Editor Harris printed only one issue of *Publick Occurrences* because it "contained reflections of a very high nature," and the next newspaper printed in Boston did not appear for fourteen years. John Campbell, a postmaster, printed and distributed the *News-Letter*, which was often only a single sheet and sometimes a half-sheet, with two columns of print. It was published "by authority" and contained nothing to disturb the government. In 1719 Campbell was removed from the post office, and was so indignant that he refused to send his paper through the mail. The new postmaster, William Brooker, began a paper called the Boston *Gazette*.

On December 22, 1719, Andrew Bradford, Postmaster of Philadelphia, began publication of the *American Weekly Mercury*. On January 2, 1721, he published this paragraph: "Our General Assembly are now sitting, and we have great expectations from them, at this juncture, that they will find some effectual remedy to revive the dying credit of this Province, and restore us to our former happy circumstances." Bradford was called before the Provincial Council to account for his words. He said the paragraph was written and inserted in the paper without his knowledge, and he was let go with a reprimand.

Years later Benjamin Franklin wrote material for the *American Weekly Mercury* which he signed "Busy Body." Near the time of an annual election he wrote a paragraph, thus signed, which said, among other things, that no one could be a patriot unless he was "first of all possessed with a public spirit and love of country."

These words obviously held a hidden, and unpleasant meaning, for Bradford was arrested, committed to prison, and bound over to the court. Andrew Hamilton was then speaker of the Pennsylvania Assembly and participated in the prosecution of Bradford for libel against the government.

Some of the characters in this little drama, which attracted small notice at the time, were to become involved in another incident which has gone down in history as the beginning of freedom of the press in the United States. This was the John Peter Zenger trial for libel held in the state of New York in 1734.

In November 1734, Zenger was arrested on a charge of libel because of material printed in his newspaper, the New York *Weekly Journal*. The charge against him, made by Governor William Cosby, was much the same as that made against *Publick Occurrences*—that his paper tended to stir up the people, to arouse factions, tumult, and sedition among them.

Editors developed an attitude, in the years between Bradford's arrest and the trial of Zenger that newspapers should be entitled to comment on public affairs. The Zenger incident began in this way:

In 1725, William Bradford (father of Andrew Bradford of the Philadelphia *Mercury*) began publication of the New York *Gazette* in that state. His son had been in trouble with authorities in Pennsylvania because of the *Mercury*, but the *Gazette* was the official organ of the New York Government.

Governor William Cosby was appointed by the crown to take the place of Governor John Montgomery, who had died suddenly in July 1731. He arrived and took over the duties of the office in August 1732. He was not particularly interested in the welfare of the people, but in making as much money as possible out of his office. Before coming to this country he had collected £6407.18.10 in perquisites, and when he arrived here, attempted to collect more.

Rip Van Dam, a New York merchant and senior member of the provincial Council, had acted as governor before the arrival of Cosby. There was a tradition that such a temporary official would pay half of the salary he had received for his services to the incoming official. This Van Dam refused to do—unless, as he suggested, Cosby would give *him* half of the £6407.18.10 he had collected in England.

Van Dam was a powerful man, and his defiance of Cosby won him a certain amount of popular support. When it became clear that Cosby was intent on lining his own pockets, other prominent New Yorkers united with Van Dam against him. One of the first strong actions against him was to launch a newspaper, The New York *Weekly Journal,* as their voice, with John Peter Zenger as editor.

The *Journal* was frankly an anti-administration newspaper. It published essays which ranged from discussions of public policy and administration to vicious personal attacks on Cosby and his circle. It also printed advertisements, many of which were thinly disguised abuses of the governor. One of them described Cosby as a monkey, and another referred to his publicist, Francis Harrison, as a dog. The *Journal* had both domestic and foreign news, much of which displeased Cosby.

William Bradford's *Gazette,* in return, printed a number of articles explaining the position of government toward criticism. It soon descended to more direct attacks.

There were, at this time, no statutes as to seditious libel in the New York laws, but it was generally conceded that English laws were in effect. In England, as the *Gazette* reminded its readers, a man could not be prevented from saying what he thought, but he must expect to suffer the consequences of his action.

Cosby tried, without success, to get the New York grand jury to take action against Zenger and his *Journal* in January 1734. The jurists refused to act, and in November, when the next grand jury sat, Chief Justice James De Lancey, acting for Governor Cosby, tried again. This time the jury considered two scandalous songs written to celebrate a victory of the Van Dam forces, but the jury refused to act, saying it was impossible to discover the author, printer, or publisher of the broadsides on which the songs were published.

Cosby persuaded the Council to request the state Assembly to order four copies of the *Journal* burned publicly. When the Assembly refused, the Council ordered that the four *Journals* be burned and that Zenger be arrested. On November 17 Zenger was put in jail.

A legal battle between Cosby and his opponents began immediately. Lewis Morris, of the Van Dam group, went to London to argue its case before officials of the crown. James Alexander and William Smith, lawyers in the Van Dam group, charged that two Supreme Court justices, De Lancey and Frederick Philipse, held office illegally. De Lancey had Alexander and Smith disbarred on April 18.

Feeling in New York was already strong against Cosby, and it was inflamed by the disbarring of the lawyers, and also by the fact that Zenger was kept in jail. Zenger had been granted bail of £400, which was excessively high though his backers could no doubt have raised that amount. It is suggested by Stanley Nider Katz, in his introduction to *A Brief Narrative of the Case and Trial of John Peter Zenger*, published by The John Harvard Library in 1963, that Zenger's supporters realized that keeping Zenger in jail made him a martyr in the eyes of the people and was therefore very helpful to their cause.

Zenger appealed to the court to appoint a lawyer for him on the same day the two men who might have been expected to defend him were disbarred. The court appointed John Chambers, a competent lawyer but a supporter of Governor Cosby. James Alexander, realizing that Chambers would not be satisfactory, appealed to Andrew Hamilton of Philadelphia to defend Zenger.

No better person could have been found. Hamilton was considered the best lawyer in America, he had had considerable experience in fighting the proprietary governor of Pennsylvania, and he had not forgotten his battle with William Bradford's son, Andrew Bradford. Oddly enough, he had fought against the younger Bradford's right to criticize the established government, and was now to fight *for* Zenger's right to do the same thing.

Zenger's trial opened on August 4, 1735, eight months after he had been arrested. The issue, from the viewpoint of Chief Justice De Lancey and Attorney-General Richard Bradley, and the accepted laws of the land, was clear. Any publication, whether true or false in its allegations, which contained written censure upon public men for their conduct as such, or upon the laws, or upon the institutions of the country, and tended to bring the government into disrepute, was committing libel. In such cases, the jury could decide only on matters of fact—that is, whether the person charged had done what he was accused of doing. If it was agreed that he had, then the judge would decide upon the punishment.

There was no question of Zenger's guilt. He was the acknowledged editor of the *Journal* and the *Journal* had published material which was extremely critical of Cosby and his administration.

Hamilton made no attempt to persuade the court that Zenger was innocent of the charges against him. Addressing the jury, which he knew was sympathetic, he argued what has been called "very bad law" (for the time), but a very popular sentiment.

He insisted that falsehood "makes a libel," and that if a thing were true it was obviously not libel. He said that "where matter of law is complicated with matter of fact" the jury have a right to determine both. They were, he said, to decide for themselves whether the statements made in the *Journal* were true or false. Otherwise, he contended, any judge, anywhere, could arbitrarily deprive anyone of his freedom.

One of Hamilton's main points was that citizens had the right to criticize their rulers. While this might not be practical in England, the government in America was closer to the people and should be conducted differently. American citizens had a legal right to protest their wrongs to their own government, but this right was useless when the government was prejudiced against them. If this failed, they had the right to carry their appeal to England, but this was such an expensive and time-consuming project that few could do it. Therefore, they must have the right to speak their minds, and juries must have the right Cosby's court would deny them—to decide on matters of law as well as on matters of fact.

"Jurymen," he said, "are to see with their own eyes, to hear with their own ears, and to make use of their own consciences and understandings, in judging of the lives, liberties, or estates of their fellow subjects."

As every student of American history knows, the jury followed Hamilton's advice and found Zenger not guilty. Oddly enough, his supporters feted Andrew Hamilton at the Black Horse Tavern the night of August 4, but Zenger was not present. He remained in jail until the next day.

The Zenger trial had no immediate effect on the laws in New York, nor was it ever cited and accepted as a precedent in libel cases. Cosby remained governor until his death in 1736 and Councilor George Clarke, one of his principal advisers, was appointed to succeed him. Zenger continued to publish the *Journal* until his death. His wife ran it for a while and then turned it over to their son, John Zenger, who published it until 1752, when it ceased from lack of paid subscriptions.

In spite of this, Zenger and his *Journal* had an effect on the growing spirit of democracy in America. The trial illustrated and made public an attitude that became more and more powerful— that ordinary citizens had the right to speak up and be heard about government.

In 1765, the first suggestion that America should separate from England appeared in print. It is credited to John Morin Scott, a New York lawyer, and was printed in the New-York *Gazette or the Weekly Post-Boy*. It said, "If then the interest of the Mother Country and her Colonies cannot be made to coincide (which I verily believe they may) if the same Constitution may not take Place in both, (as it certainly ought to do), if the Welfare of the Mother Country, necessarily requires a Sacrifice of the most valuable natural Rights of the Colonies Their Right of making their own

Laws and Disposing of their own Property by Representatives of their own choosing;—if such is really the Case between Great-Britain and her Colonies, then the Connection between them ought to cease. . . ."

Frederick Hudson, in *Journalism in America,* says, "There were 37 papers published in the United States on the commencement of the Revolutionary War in 1775: with them began the independence of the Nation."

Many of these papers did not resemble what we would consider an ideal newspaper today. They were frankly biased; often the only reason for their publication was to persuade others to their way of thinking. Their news was scanty, often late, and many times inaccurate. Their publication was irregular (publishers were always having to cease publication from lack of money) and the number of subscribers was small.

After our own government was established, our common laws provided that truth was no defense in case of libel, the judge decided upon matters of intent, the jury was confined to questions of fact, and punishment was left to the discretion of the court.

In 1798, the Alien and Sedition Laws were passed by the Federalist party because of its fear of the growing strength of the Republican party led by Thomas Jefferson, the intemperate and slanderous attacks made upon the government by Republican newspapers, and the "foreign menace" represented by French agents, refugees, and other aliens.

The Alien and Sedition Acts allowed the President to deport aliens he considered dangerous. It also prohibited the publication of any false, scandalous, or malicious writings which would bring the government, Congress, or the President into contempt or disrepute, excite popular hostility to them, incite resistance to the laws of the United States, or encourage hostile designs against the United States. Safeguards were included in which truth was admitted as a defense in case of slander and libel, proof of malicious intent was required, the jury was permitted to determine questions of law as well as of fact, and limits were placed on the amount of fines and the term of imprisonment which could be imposed.

Of the 200 newspapers being published in 1798 in this country, 20 or 25 were opposed to the administration and were also edited by aliens. Only about 25 people were indicted under the Sedition Act and hardly a dozen of these were brought to trial. Matthew Lyon, a Republican congressman from Vermont, was convicted of sedition, fined $1,000 and sentenced to serve four years in prison.

The safeguards were more liberal than the common laws of the time, and yet most of the newspapers of America rushed to the defense of those opposing the government and called the period a "Reign of Terror." They insisted that the new Acts were in defiance of the Constitution and were for the sole purpose of preventing Americans from criticizing their own government. The Alien Act expired on June 25, 1800; and the life of the Sedition Act terminated on March 3, 1801. In 1964, the Supreme Court, in reversing the libel decision against the New York *Times* mentioned in the last chapter, also branded the Sedition Act of 1798 as unconstitutional.

Those of us who are proud of being Americans, whether we are newspaper people or not, want to see our way of life preserved. Yet history has established the fact that most of us feel the best way to maintain it is to criticize it freely.

8. The President and the Press

". . . he said he despised their attacks on him, personally, but there had never been an act of the government, not meaning in the executive line only, but in every line, which that paper had not abused." Thomas Jefferson, speaking of President George Washington.

****

CBS News Photo

President Kennedy with reporters from major radio and television networks.

THE GREATEST SERVICE a free press can perform for a free people is to act as a constant check on the government and government officials. We have never had a President or an administration which has not been freely criticized in various newspapers throughout the country.

George Washington was our only President to be elected unanimously by the Electoral College. He was certainly the most respected and best-liked American of his time, and yet he was hardly inaugurated when newspaper attacks on him began. When his term of office ended, the *Aurora* of Philadelphia said, "The man who is the source of all the misfortune of our country is this day reduced to a level with his fellow citizens, and is no longer possessed of power to multiply evils upon the United States . . . this day ought to be a JUBILEE in the United States."

The attacks on our second President, John Adams, and his administration, were so violent and uncontrolled that they led to the infamous Sedition Act. When Thomas Jefferson became our third President, the newspapers were so vicious that he said, "Nothing can now be believed which is seen in a newspaper. Truth itself becomes suspicious by being put into that polluted vehicle."

Many of our Presidents have had reason to agree with the *Columbian Central* which said, in 1797, "There is a liberty of the press which is very little short of the burning of our houses." In spite of that, most of them would agree with Jefferson, who said in his old age, "The only security of us all is in a free press."

Personal and political animosity accounts for much of the newspaper criticism of government. The Democratic editor who violently opposed a presidential candidate, only to see him successful, will not miss many of the mistakes he makes in office. The Republican editor who believes a Democratic administration is running a "welfare state" will continually point it out to his readers.

Aside from this, there is a very real difference of opinion between the American government and the American press.

The business of the government is running the country, and the business of the press is reporting the news. The government is one of the biggest sources of news which is of interest, or should be, to every citizen.

However, government is a very complex and difficult business. It is not always helpful to have everything that is said and done in Washington broadcast through the press. When delicate negotiations which could be damaged by comment or criticism are going on, the officials involved do not wish premature publicity. Our Defense Department conducts tests of a new weapon which it wants to keep secret, but it comes in conflict with a reporter who says, "The people who pay for these weapons have a right to know about them." Government officials, being human, make mistakes. They are certainly not eager to have them exposed in a newspaper. Who is to decide, in each case, how it will be handled? There is no law or set of regulations which governs the matter, though the government and the press have an agreement: Where the national security is involved, the press will not reveal the pertinent information, although it may be aware of it. Where the national welfare is involved, the news of our government is open to the press. This agreement is sometimes breached by one side and sometimes by the other, but it is generally observed.

There are often differences of opinion between the press and the government as to any particular situation. The government may insist that revealing certain facts at a specific time will be injurious to our national welfare, while the press may contend that the publication of those very facts at that very time is essential to our well-being. Every newspaper believes that it knows what is best for the country, and so does every official, so there is bound to be conflict.

This conflict often centers around the President, because he is the head of the government. Some Presidents have tried to tame the great force of the press, and some have tried to best it in battle. No one has wholly succeeded, and no one has wholly failed.

The problem is more acute today because of the speed with which news travels. When George Washington was inaugurated, it took the news two days to travel from New York to Philadelphia, and weeks to reach more distant parts of the country. Today every one in the United States and the rest of the world knows about it very quickly. The voter who disapproves of an act of the President can send him a telegram immediately. Years ago it would have been weeks before he learned of it, and weeks before his comment could reach the White House.

News from our capital has always been sought by newspapers, and by 1892 there were about 150 correspondents sending regular news dispatches from there. A number of the larger papers had their own Washington bureaus.

President McKinley is credited with the "invention" of the press conference. He occasionally called several reporters together to make a public statement for the papers and sometimes gave other news to groups of reporters. President Theodore Roosevelt set aside an anteroom in the White House for correspondents and sometimes called as many as fifty of them to his desk for an important announcement. When he wanted to test public opinion of a proposed action he gave out news in the form of a "trial balloon" to see what the reaction would be. President Taft originated a policy of weekly press conferences to which all accredited correspondents were invited, and at which questions might be asked. He could not be quoted directly, but a reporter might write, "The President believes that. . . ."

President Woodrow Wilson was not especially happy in his relations with the press and held only irregular and widely spaced press conferences. When World War I began he abandoned them completely, and newsmen were forced to rely on his private secretary for their releases. President Harding made an unwise statement in a press conference, and its widespread publication embarrassed him so much that he later required that all questions be submitted in advance, in writing. President Coolidge also answered only previously submitted questions, as did President Hoover.

President Franklin Roosevelt held news conferences in his office, but broke precedent by granting one exclusive interview, with permission to quote him directly. The storm of protest from other newsmen was so great that he never repeated it. He did, however, occasionally receive journalists privately to acquaint them with his "thinking" on matters of vital interest.

President Harry Truman gave an exclusive interview to the same correspondent of the New York *Times* who had been granted that privilege by President Roosevelt, and again the storm of protest arose. After that, he ruled that the results of any such interview be veiled behind references to "a source close to the President," or some other such journalistic device.

President Eisenhower all but eliminated the controversial element of special treatment of individual reporters. His attitude toward the press may be indicated by a statement he is quoted as having made to his Cabinet: "Anyone who has time to listen to commentators or read columnists obviously doesn't have enough work to do."

President John F. Kennedy brought an entirely different attitude to the presidency. He read more newspapers regularly than any of his predecessors and had no doubt about their importance. While still a senator he made personal friends of many newsmen, and the exclusive interviews he gave were countless.

The presidential press conferences were moved from the old Indian Treaty Room where they had been held by President Truman to a large auditorium in the State Department where as many as 500 reporters might gather. Conferences were telecast live so that the whole country might view his give-and-take with reporters.

The staff of press relations people at the White House was larger than ever before in history, and newsmen were at home there as they have rarely been during other administrations.

While much of the press and the public enjoyed this state of affairs, there was another side to the picture. Veteran reporters saw grave dangers in the situation. A newsman who is too close to the presidency with all of its burdens and problems and who also thinks of the President as a personal friend, is not apt to be very objective when writing about the administration. President Kennedy let reporters and editors know what he thought of their stories, so that his opinions were used as a kind of censorship. Those who valued his friendship, it was charged, would hesitate before writing a story, however true, that might damage the relationship.

On April 2, 1962, the magazine *U. S. News & World Report* published a lengthy report on the Kennedy "image" and how it was being built. The article said individual reporters were wooed by personal interviews with the President and punished by criticism of unfavorable stories. Sometimes offenders were shut off from regular news sources. Publishers were entertained regularly at the White House in a series of luncheons designed to include representatives of the press from all over the country. Press secretaries of governors of states were called to Washington for private talks about presidential goals and practices. Reporters, columnists and commentators were high on the White House guest list. A survey showed that an average of one out of every five guests at presidential luncheons and dinners was a writer or reporter.

In the late summer of 1962, we had a showdown with Cuba over missile bases supplied by Russia to them. It was a tense and dangerous situation that could have led to war. When it was over, the press almost unanimously praised President Kennedy for his handling of a difficult situation.

Shortly after that, the American press exploded. Charges were made that reporters had been denied information during the crisis and also that they had been given misleading information. On October 29, Arthur Sylvester, Assistant Secretary of Defense, admitted publicly that the government had been using "management" and "control" over news as a "weapon." He described news as "part of the weaponry that a President has in the application of military force and related forces to the solution of political problems, or to the application of internal political pressure." He also said, "In the kind of world we live in, the generation of news by action taken by the Government becomes one weapon in a strained situation. The results, in my opinion, justify the methods we used."

Regulations governing news at the State Department gave rise to more criticism. An official approached for an interview or information by a newsman could agree, *if* he was authorized, *if* the information was not "classified," *if* an official colleague was also present, and/or *if* the subject discussed was made known at once to the office of the Assistant Secretary of State.

Newsmen who accept necessary restrictions on information relating to our national security felt that this was going entirely too far. The Washington *Evening Star* said in an editorial about the Cuban crisis, "No newspaper correspondents were permitted on the scene. The traditional facilities usually supplied for that purpose were denied, for reasons obviously phony. So Mr. Sylvester and his cohorts—carrying out orders, we are sure—were left in control of what was to be printed.

"It subsequently was revealed that only those portions of the news were made available by Mr. Sylvester which he and other omniscient manipulators of public opinion decided, in their infinite wisdom, would best serve to create the 'image' of this country's activities they wish to manufacture and place before our people and the world.

". . . Mr. Sylvester may have overlooked one likely result of 'the methods we used.' The result is that Mr. Sylvester and his superiors, from this time on, are suspect. . . . What they say . . . may be the truth. But that truth will be accepted with a grain of salt."

Other papers were more violent in their language. An editorial protesting "management" of news from the Honolulu *Star Bulletin* was read into the Congressional Record. In March 1963 the fires were still blazing. Arthur Krock of the New York *Times* published an article in *Fortune* magazine which contained extremely strong criticism. He said, "A news management not only exists, but, in the form of *direct* and *deliberate* action, has been enforced more cynically and boldly than by any previous administration in a period when the U.S. was not in a war or without visible means of regression from the verge of war." After listing various ways in which the news, and the people who gather and write it, were being influenced, Mr. Krock came to a rather surprising conclusion. He said that the newspapers and those who write them were to blame if their coverage of the news was influenced.

Let us consider for a moment that President Kennedy was one of the most powerful Presidents in our history. He had immense personal popularity and prestige, he headed the larger of our two political parties, he was brilliant, charming, and effective. The international situation was such as to give him unusual powers which he would not have had in a more peaceful era. If his critics were to be believed, he used every available resource to control and influence the American press. In spite of this, Mr. Krock blamed the press for what success the President had.

His summation of the situation clearly defines the continuing battle between our government and the press. He said, in effect, that it is the job of newsmen to get the news. What the government says, does, or is, may make the job harder, but it is no excuse for failure.

This struggle between the government and the press is the best safeguard for our freedoms. A government which controlled a subservient press or a press which honored no restraints on what it printed—either could be the end of democracy.

9.

Propaganda and the Press

"Why should freedom of speech and freedom of the press be allowed? Why should a government which is doing what it believes to be right allow itself to be criticized? It would not allow opposition by lethal weapons. Ideas are much more fatal than guns. Why should any man be allowed to buy a printing press and disseminate pernicious opinions calculated to embarrass the government? Nikolai Lenin: Speech in Moscow, 1920.

****

Wide World Photo

WITH MUSTARD—AND RELISH: Nelson A. Rockefeller takes his campaign into a delicatessen. On right is Attorney General Louis J. Lefkowitz.

grants freedom of the press to the Russian people. Article 125 of that Constitution says, ". . . the citizens of the USSR are granted by law . . . freedom of the press . . . and these civil rights are ensured by placing at the disposal of the working people and their organizations printing presses, stocks of paper . . . and other materials to exercise these rights." Elsewhere it says that all freedoms are granted the Russian people "in conformity with the interests of the working people, and to strengthen the socialist system." The last sentence defines the limits of the free press in Russia.

The "working people" are considered as a whole, and not as individuals. The representatives of the working people are members of the Communist party, and the leaders of the Communist party regulate the Russian press for what they decide are the best interests of the people.

The Russian press is not a goad on the government as ours is, but a tool of the government. The newspapers are not merely controlled to be sure they print what the government wishes, but they are used as an army might be used to advance the cause of the state.

This is a different concept of the use of the press, and is the opposite of our own. It is one of four major concepts of mass communication, as defined by Tyrus Butler of the University of Georgia's School of Journalism.

The first concept of a controlled press is that of a censored press. In this concept, newspapers are allowed, but what they may print is controlled by the government. This control may take the form of censorship which is done *after* the newspaper is printed, but has the effect of preventing papers from printing material which might create trouble with the government. For example, at the time of the recent Algerian crises in France, newspapers were shut down by the government. On February 17, 1961, the major French press federations or press associations protested seizures of whole editions of newspapers which were deemed to contain material in opposition to government policy.

Another form of censorship, and a more extreme one, is licensing of the press. Only papers licensed by the government may be printed, and licenses are granted only to those whose support of the government is assured.

The purpose of censoring the press is to make certain that nothing displeasing to the government is printed.

The second concept is that of the press used as a tool of the government, where its contents are deliberately written for the purpose of furthering the aims of the government. In this concept, the state is more important than the individual. What best serves the interests of the state is best for everyone, and the individual has no rights which might conflict with the state.

The third concept is one that struggled for existence in early America—that of complete freedom from government censorship. During the sixteenth and seventeenth centuries the idea that the people had the right to know began to develop. John Locke said that power belongs to the people, and they should have the sort of government they wish. Therefore, they have the right to individual freedom of thought and action so that they can create a government best suited to the interests of all.

John Peter Zenger and his supporters believed that his paper had the right to criticize the government of New York. Other early American newspapers believed they had the right to criticize the governments of their states, and of England. Our newspapers, as we have seen, insist on this right today.

The fourth concept is an outgrowth of the third. It is that the press should be free to print, and that it should also be free to *know*. Zenger, in spite of his courage and liberal ideas, would hardly have dared insist that he be present to report the exact happenings of a conference between Governor Cosby and his assistants. He was not so concerned with getting the exact facts of both sides of every controversy, as of being free to print his side.

Our newspapers are continually waging a battle to have all sources of information open to them, and at the same time they are concerned with arriving at and presenting to their readers *all* of the facts and not one portion of them. The fourth concept might then be called the fully informed and responsible press.

We are quick to call the news that appears in the controlled press "propaganda," because it is not written to inform, but to influence. This is so whether it is true or not. A news story in a totalitarian country might say that the country's production of tractors was the largest in history, and cite the facts to prove it. It might well not say that the workers who manufactured them earned starvation wages, that the materials used were inferior and the tractors themselves inefficient.

Does propaganda ever appear in our newspapers? It does indeed. Many candidates for high office in our country are wealthy men. During the campaign, you will see pictures of them engaged in warm, friendly, informal activities. They will be shown eating hot-dogs, holding babies, talking with farmers in front of the post office, and perhaps hunting or fishing. These pictures say, "This candidate is not a stiff, haughty, proud rich man, but one of US," no matter what the caption underneath may read. Some propaganda is as innocuous as this, but some is not.

Noted people, politicians, organizations, government bureaus, and thousands of others have publicity agents who feed reams of material about them to the press. Though this material is carefully rationed by editors, a great deal of it appears in print. Perhaps we should watch with a critical eye any news that deals with politicians, since their actions in public office can have such a strong effect on our lives.

One of the most popular types of propaganda for politicians might be called the "All-American." Each candidate for public office would have us believe that he, and not his opponent, will promote the finest ideals of our country. This is an admirable goal, but just what does a particular politician mean? His voting record, his actions in public life, and his speeches are a good indication of whether his viewpoint about America is one worthy of support.

Another propaganda device is the "glittering generality." Most candidates are in favor of government economy, world peace, raising America's stature, lowering taxes, and providing more jobs. The important thing is *how* they intend to achieve these goals and what their record shows about their ability to do it.

"Name-calling" can be extremely effective, both for and against others. The Russian press, for example, frequently refers to us as "imperialistic war-mongers" and to themselves as "peace-mongers." It became the fashion a few years ago to refer to certain people in government as "egg-heads," implying that they were impractical intellectuals, and out of step with the rest of the country.

"The plain-folks device" abounds in political circles. Candidates, regardless of their background, social position or economic status, are inclined to dress informally when campaigning. "I am one of you," the candidate is saying, "aware of your problems and sympathetic to your needs. Sending me to Washington will give you a friend with the power to help you."

"Card-stacking" is a way of telling the truth, but not all of the truth. A candidate may point with horror at the record of unemployment in the country during the administration of the opposing party, without referring to the unemployment when his party was in office. He may select one issue, such as lowering taxes, and make it seem the very salvation of the American voter, without explaining that it may also mean cutting down on government services to the people.

"Get on the band-wagon." Every politician tries to make it appear that he is much more popular than his opponent, and that his policies are exactly what the public wants. Most people have a tendency to want to go with the crowd, and if they are convinced that the majority want a certain candidate or party, they will tend to support it (or fail to speak up for their own preferences for fear of criticism).

The purpose underlying all propaganda is to influence, rather than to inform. The more effective it is, the more it arouses emotions instead of thought. It is perhaps well to beware of any statement or news story that makes an immediate and strong appeal to the emotions and to check the facts it contains.

This is not to say that propaganda is bad in itself. Sometimes our emotions must be involved before our minds become interested.

Propaganda has been used to help some of the best causes we have and will always be put to use when men communicate with each other.

Many a newspaperman has the instincts of a reformer, and makes good use of his pen to affect the public welfare. Jacob Augustus Riis, reporter on the New York *Sun*, author and social reformer, was such a man. Lincoln Steffens, in *McClure's Magazine,* said this of him: "If any rich man could mark a city with as many good works as Jacob A. Riis has thrust upon New York, his name would be called good and great. . . . Riis did the work that won small parks for bad spots in our city; he labored years for enough schools; he made himself great. . . . Riis is a reporter. The evils he exposed he discovered as a reporter (for the *Sun*); as a reporter he wrung men's hearts with them; and the reporter with his 'roasts' compelled indifferent city officials to concede the reforms he suggested or approved. Consider these reforms: It was Riis who exposed the contaminated state of the city's water supply, and thus brought about the purchase of the whole Croton watershed. It was Riis who forced the destruction of rear tenements, and thus relieved the hideous darkness and density of life among the poor. It was the reporter with his nagging that wiped out Mulberry Bend, the worst tenement block in the city, and had the space turned into a park. . . . Riis fought for and secured a truant school; he demanded light for dark tenement hallways, got it, and thus opened one hiding place of vice, crime and filth. He worked for the abolition of child labor, and, when a law was enacted, compelled its enforcement. Playgrounds for schools and the opening of school rooms to boys' and girls' clubs were of his work."

We would all agree that Riis used propaganda to good effect for a good purpose. Totalitarian governments use the press for propaganda and tell their people it is the truth; when our government or any group or individual attempts to use our press for propaganda, it is up to us to see it for what it is.

10. The Changing Concept of News

"There was no news because there were no real newspapers." *AP—
The Story of News,* Oliver Gramling.

****

Wide World Photo

Diagram shows how the first tv program, beamed directly from Europe to the U. S., was relayed the night of July 11, 1962, by Telstar satellite from a French station to Andover, Maine. Telstar was over the Atlantic Ocean between Newfoundland and Europe at the time of the telecast.

NEWS, AS WE THINK OF IT, is a fairly modern development. Those who fought to establish freedom of the press in America were actually fighting for freedom of expression and not merely for freedom to print the news. Some commentators have said, like Mr. Gramling, that early newspapers in America had no news in them.

America's first newspaper, *Publick Occurrences,* 1690, contained a series of brief, gossipy paragraphs which were supposedly accounts of the latest happenings. They were vague, and never confirmed.

"It's reported the City of *Cork* in *Ireland* has proclaimed K. *William,* and turned their *French* landlords out of doors: of this there wants further confirmation."

"The Christianized *Indians* in some parts of *Plimouth,* have newly appointed a day of Thanksgiving to God for his mercy in supplying their extream and pinching Necessities under their late want of Corn, and for His giving them now a prospect of a very *Comfortable Harvest.* Their example may be worth mentioning."

It is obvious that this sort of news story is based almost entirely on rumor, that the editor heard it as it passed from person to person, and that it may or may not be true. A trained newsman who had been at the scene of either event would have written a story much different from either of these.

The first independent newspapers in America, and for many years afterward, existed for a main purpose other than that of printing the news. They were used by patriots to arouse Americans against British rule and to bind them into one people. Later newspapers were usually violently partisan (either for one political party or another, or for or against some particular cause). Their contents were intended to instruct and influence the public, and what news they carried was simply an added ingredient.

In many cases no real attempt was made to check its accuracy. Stories of the wildest nature made their appearance in the most respectable newspapers, with no apology from the editor. "A farmer in Virginia is said to have a calf with 8 legs, a face like a dog, and covered with fur like a bear." "Travellers in Arkansas report a snake in that area called the Hoop Snake which rolls itself into a hoop with its tail in its mouth and rolls rapidly away when pursued."

The appearance of newspapers, even as late as a hundred years ago, was quite different from those of today. The front page rarely carried large headlines, but almost always contained advertisements. (Some of the things advertised might be as unreliable as some of the news.) Along with accounts of recent happenings, the front page normally included a few educational paragraphs which might tell about the scenery in France, the method of raising grapes in Spain, and how to avoid railroad accidents. There might be a poem or two, and perhaps part or all of a sermon preached recently by a local minister.

The rest of the paper was much the same. During times of great excitement there would be columns of news about the current issues or events, interspersed with what we would think of as "fillers." The news accounts were sometimes written by reporters or editors, but often they were reprints from other papers, or the contents of letters received by the editor. Much of the news of the Civil War came to local papers by way of letters from local people engaged in the war. Since the letter writers were not trained reporters, and since most army camps are rumor factories, many of the stories printed about the war were highly inaccurate.

A good editor could do a good job of covering the news in his vicinity, but what was considered news was different then. The first copy of the *Concord Daily Monitor* printed in Concord, New Hampshire, on May 23, 1864, contained only one story about an event in Concord, a musical concert; the rest of its news columns were filled with reports from the state government and the Civil War. It considered announcements of deaths and marriages and obituaries as advertisements—not news—and listed the charges for them.

It would not be accurate to call the *Monitor,* or any other one paper, typical of all papers of its time, because newspapers differed from one another even more than they do now. It is not accurate to say that no newspapers recognized and printed what we think of as news today, because efforts in that direction had begun as early as 1811. Each newspaper was shaped by its editor's purpose and ideas, and limited by the difficulties of obtaining a fresh and adequate supply of accurate news.

In 1811, in Boston, the Exchange Coffee House opened a Reading Room for its patrons. The room supplied whatever newspapers were available, and its proprietor, Samuel Gilbert, had two large ledgers in which he entered the latest marine intelligence and general information. The books contained considerably more news than any of the papers.

Mr. Samuel Topliff, Jr., took over the management of the news-books, as they were called, and began to improve their contents. Patrons of the Reading Room had donated a rowboat with which

Gilbert sometimes met incoming boats in the harbor to get fresh news, and Topliff began to use it regularly. His patrons were so pleased that he employed correspondents to send him regular newsletters from abroad which he could add to his books. Eventually he persuaded a few newspapers to subscribe to regular reports which he wrote out in longhand and delivered by messenger or stagecoach. (This was not a new idea. Enterprising men had circulated news in the form of private letters in both America and Europe for many years. Topliff differed from his predecessors in his efforts to get a wide variety of fresh, accurate, and reliable news circulated as widely as possible.)

In large cities the idea of news as an economic asset to a newspaper grew rapidly. By 1828, the competition between newspapers in New York for news was intense. When the *Journal of Commerce,* owned by merchant-philanthropist Arthur Tappan and managed by 37-year-old David Hale, was founded, it brought the number of New York newspapers to ten. The newcomer in the field found it almost impossible to get news of incoming ships. This news included some from the foreign lands where the ship had been, as well as information about cargoes, shipments, market prices, and other sailings. Boatmen from the *Journal of Commerce* were beaten over the head with belaying pins by competing newsmen as they climbed up ships' ladders. They returned to the *Journal* with their heads laid open, but no news.

Just before Tappan decided to sell his paper, Hale fitted out a sloop which sailed down the East River eighteen miles to Sandy Hook, where incoming ships paused to trim their sails. The opposition newspapers fitted out their own sloop and a race ensued, but no blood was shed. As the *Journal of Commerce* said, "An opportu-

86

nity will now be offered by honorable competition. The public will be benefitted by such extra exertions to procure marine news, and we trust the only contention between the two boat establishments will be which can outdo the other in vigilance, perseverance and success. . . ."

Daniel Craig, a New Hampshire man, used carrier pigeons to carry ship news. He met ships miles out at sea, summarized the news from abroad, and sent it winging back to shore by the pigeons. Newspapers in Boston, New York, and Baltimore subscribed to his "pigeon post."

David Hale printed New York's first "extra" by running off important news for distribution during the afternoon. He broke precedent by putting the most important news on page one. His paper proudly announced its fresh foreign news with the by-line "25 DAYS LATER FROM EUROPE." A pony express was inaugurated for the fast transmission of news from its source to the newspaper.

James Gordon Bennett started his famous *New York Herald* on May 6, 1835, and with it, a new concept of news. He is often credited with having "invented" news as we know it today, because he gave his readers information in so many areas which had not been previously considered suitable for newspaper publication. He promised that he would print the inside story of everything that happened, and to the astonishment and often dismay of the world, he did so.

He reported in detail on public occurrences, the proceedings of public meetings, and the happenings in the world of crime. He originated the practice of interviewing prominent people, and gave his readers lurid, dramatic and exciting views of the city around them. His paper reeked of sensationalism, scandal, murder, and horror, but its circulation grew by leaps and bounds. Even those who disapproved of him and of his paper read it, and in spite of his own great personal unpopularity, the fashion he had begun spread to other papers.

Bennett did much to change the contents of newspapers and is credited with having published the first Wall Street report on May 11, 1835, with having pioneered in a new plan of distributing newspapers through agencies, with establishing the "cash" system of purchase as opposed to subscriptions, with printing summaries of news, with having printed the first newspaper war map, and with having started the practice of using foreign correspondents. He also printed sermons and religious news as well as political speeches.

New developments in transportation and communications made the rapid transmission of news possible, and every new development was put to work for newspapers. In 1848 an office was opened at Broadway and Liberty Street in New York, as headquarters for the Associated Press. The entire cost of operations for the first year was less than $20,000. Foreign news was purchased, but domestic news was sent to the main office by telegraph. Those who supplied the news were known as agents, and their job was not only to gather news but to telegraph it in.

The new Associated Press covered its first presidential election—between Zachary Taylor, Whig; Lewis Cass, Democrat; and Martin Van Buren, Free Soil. It covered the Gold Rush in California, the battles of Garibaldi, and the latest census returns. Stories that came in were duplicated on tissue paper and delivered to member papers by messenger.

News had become a big thing. Americans began to feel entitled to know all about every important event very soon after it happened. Newspapers began to be what the name implied, instead of purveyors of personal or political opinion with a bit of news thrown in.

The rotary press made it possible to print more papers faster. (Most early papers with hand presses had circulations of only a few hundred, since a strong pressman could run off only about 200 copies an hour.) The first transatlantic cable brought Europe within immediate reach. In 1884 typewriters came into use in newspaper offices, and in 1901 Marconi demonstrated the practical use of wireless.

About this time, Charles L. Krum and his son Howard perfected an automatic machine to send the printed word by wire without the use of code. They called it the Morkrum Telegraph Printer. A sending operator sat at a keyboard similar to that of an ordinary typewriter and typed out a news dispatch. The machine perforated a paper tape with a series of holes, each combination representing a letter. The tape fed a boxlike transmitter which transformed the tape perforations into electrical impulses and sent them along the wires into receiving offices miles away. These impulses actuated telegraph keys and set the receiving machines automatically reproducing the original letters. The lineal descendants of the Morkrum Telegraph Printer are the teletypes used in newspaper offices today.

In 1960, *The Working Press of the Nation,* a newspaper directory, listed 38 different wire services which supply news throughout the world from every source and covering every subject. These services make use of every known form of transportation and communication device to get the latest news from wherever it happens to the pages of our local newspapers within a matter of hours.

The great revolution in news took place in less than two hundred years. The one issue of *Publick Occurrences,* of September 25, 1690, was content to print rumor and gossip from the street and coffee houses. At the beginning of the nineteenth century newsmen were finding better methods of bringing news to the papers, and by the end of that century newsmen were going all over the world to where the news happened so that they could report it accurately.

11. Pictures in the Press

"A picture may instantly present what a book could set forth only in a hundred pages." Ivan Turgenev in *Fathers and Sons*.

****

Syndicated cartoon by Fischetti, 1965.

IN 1835 JAMES GORDON BENNETT
published the first newspaper picture used to illustrate a current
news story. It showed the old Merchant's Exchange in New York
which had burned down that year, or so the caption said. Newspaper presses were so poorly adapted to the reproduction of pictures
that it was often difficult to tell exactly what they showed. When
Bennett printed what was called a drawing of General Jackson's
funeral, in 1845, his rivals made wild fun of him. They insisted
that the same blurred, smudgy, foggy drawing had been used to
illustrate Queen Victoria's Coronation, the funeral of General William Henry Harrison, and the Croton Water Celebration.

It was possible to reproduce excellent pictures by lithography,
and Nathaniel Currier (of the Currier and Ives prints) was in the
business of publishing realistic drawings of current events from the
year 1840 on. They were sold independently, as a separate thing
from newspapers, and their success made it clear that the public
was interested in "seeing" the news as well as reading it.

The first actual news pictures of a major war story are thought to
be daguerreotypes taken of United States staff officers and troops
during the Mexican war. They were not used in newspapers at the
time, but a series of drawings was prepared at the direction of
George Wilkins Kendall, the only reporter who accompanied the
American army, and these were printed in newspapers.

Frank Leslie's Illustrated Newspaper, founded in 1855, and
Harper's Weekly, founded in 1857, made generous use of line
drawings to illustrate stories, but daily newspapers considered such
things unsuited to their purposes. (They did not consider either of
the above as true newspapers, but as magazines.) Newspapers did
use war maps, which were eagerly studied by their readers, during

the Civil War. The photographs by Matthew B. Brady which made the actual scenes of the war itself so vivid were sold to the public to supplement the news, not as newspaper illustrations.

The New York *Daily Graphic,* in 1873, was the first American daily to use illustrations regularly. Because of technical limitations, they were black and white line drawings. The few papers that adopted the practice did so only sparingly, and months might intervene between the appearance of one illustration and the next.

It was not until March 14, 1880, that the first halftone photograph appeared in a newspaper. It was not excellent, but it reproduced the various shades of gray which make up a photograph.

Joseph Pulitzer used line drawings from woodcuts to illustrate the news in his daily New York *World* and circulation jumped. He felt it was undignified, however, and ordered the woodcuts to be gradually eliminated. Circulation began to drop and the order was rescinded. Other newspapers saw the trend and by the eighties news pictures were well established as part of newspapers.

Today photo-journalism is almost as much a part of news as the words with which news stories are written. Pictures of events appear on television, in news magazines, and in our newspapers so often that we today do not realize how drab the newspapers of early times looked. The presence of photographs on the scene helps us to have a sense of close participation in current events.

There is an old truism that "the camera never lies," but this is far from true. News pictures, like news stories, can be slanted. The appearance of a candidate for public office, because of photo-journalism, is an important factor in his success at the polls. Newspapers have been accused of publishing only "noble" pictures of their favorite candidates and embarrassing and unflattering pictures of the opposition. Photographs of actual events can be distorted by the photographer. A picture of a riot may show a rioter throwing a rock at a policeman, or it may show a policeman with a billy club poised over the head of a rioter. There is also the area of deliberate deceit in news photography where pictures are distorted by the elimination of parts of them, by combining features of two separate pictures, or by using captions which give a misleading impression, but few newspapers resort to this.

There are other pictorial features in newspapers besides photographs. Comic strips are run for the amusement of readers, and drawings are used to show the latest fashions. Charts, graphs, and maps are regular features of papers, all designed to tell us more about the world.

Editorial cartoons had their beginning in America before the Revolution. Often printed on cheap, flimsy sheets of paper called "broadsides," they depicted a current situation from a highly biased point of view. The characters shown were usually symbolic and those of the opposition were often shown with horns and a tail.

Paul Revere helped bring about our rebellion against England by cartoons printed as broadsides and distributed to the colonies. Some of them he is credited with having drawn himself, but others he is said to have copied from English broadsides which he retitled to fit the local situation.

Editorial cartoons are designed to attract readers to the editorial page and to illustrate editorial comments and attitudes. Large newspapers have their own cartoonists, while smaller ones buy cartoons from syndicates, selecting those of their own political complexion.

The purpose of an editorial cartoon is not to illustrate the news, *per se,* but to interpret it. Good cartoonists have a tremendous influence on the public.

Thomas Nast, as a cartoonist for *Harper's Weekly* and the New York *Times,* helped to overthrow Tammany Hall and routed a political group led by William M. Tweed, called "Boss" Tweed.

Many New Yorkers were aware, in the 1860's, that their city government was corrupt. Thomas Nast began a campaign by cartoon that illuminated the situation and helped destroy it. Just before the election of 1870, he published a cartoon called "The Power Behind The Throne," which showed Governor Hoffman in crown and ermine seated on a throne labeled "Tammany," flanked by others of his group. A coat of arms on a canopy above the throne displayed two tigers rampant. (In his youth, Boss Tweed ran a fire engine called the Big Six, which had a tiger as its emblem. He carried the emblem with him "for luck" when he entered politics, and Nast was eventually to use it against him in a way that shook the city.)

The second cartoon, typical of the period, was called "Our Modern Falstaff Reviewing His Army" and showed Tweed inspecting his troops—loafers, roughs, ward-heelers, jail-birds, etc. The caption read, "My whole charge consists of slaves ragged as Lazarus, and such as indeed were never soldiers, but discarded serving men and revolted tapsters. No eye hath seen such scarecrows. Nay, and the villains march wide between the legs as if they had fetters on; for, indeed, I had the most of them out of prison." Descriptive captions for some of the early cartoons were more nearly essays.

In spite of the Nast cartoons, the election was won by the Tammany forces. Tweed asked his critics, "What are you going to do about it?"

Nast had no actual proof of wrong-doing by Tweed, but he persisted in his attack.

In January 1871 he published a cartoon showing Tweed and his friends looting the public treasury. Tweed was furious and ordered that the city buy no more textbooks from the Harper firm. Nast then published a cartoon showing Tweed throwing textbooks out of a schoolroom window. On a blackboard in the background were the words, "Hoffman will be our next president." Another cartoon showed a gigantic thumb covering the whole of New York city. The cuff link above the thumb bore the name William M. Tweed. The caption was, "Well, what are you going to do about it?"

In July a disgruntled former member of the Tweed gang approached the editor of the *Times* with copies of actual financial records which showed that more than ten million dollars a day had been stolen from the city. Before the first of the records could appear in print, the editor was offered a bribe said to be in the millions, and Nast was offered an enormous sum of money to help him "complete his studies of art in Europe." Neither man accepted a bribe or stopped the campaign.

The records were published, but in spite of that top members of the Tweed gang clung to their power and tried to ride out the storm. Nast continued with his powerful cartoons. On November 11, two days before the election, he published six cartoons, one of them considered one of the finest editorial cartoons ever printed. It showed a coliseum with Tweed and his friends in the imperial box. In the arena a powerful tiger is mauling a prostrate female figure,

"The Republic." The Sword of Justice and the symbol of the ballot are broken into fragments. Under the cartoon are these words: "The Tammany Tiger—What are you going to do about it?"

In 1873 Tweed was arrested. In 1878, he died in jail. He is reported to have said to one of his friends, "It ain't the things they write about me I mind so much—it's them ——— pictures."

Many great American political cartoonists have flourished since the day of Nast, among them Ding (J. N. Darling), Harold M. Talburt, Carey Orr, Edmund Duffy, Herblock (Herbert L. Block), Art Young, Boardman Robinson, William Gropper, Robert Minor, Bill Mauldin, and others.

Editorial cartoons are perhaps not as colorful, and not as powerful, as they have been in the past, but they still exert a tremendous influence. One picture may throw a situation or a character into perspective so that a point of view is instantly clarified. *Time* in 1964 published a group of sketches of Senator Goldwater, Republican candidate for President, made by prominent cartoonists. Although each one was immediately recognizable, some made him appear to be one sort of man and some another. Cartoonists who opposed him showed him in an unsympathetic guise, his supporters showed him in a flattering way. It is obvious that readers of newspapers are affected by the particular view of people and events shown them in cartoons.

Most of our standard American symbols, Uncle Sam, the Republican elephant and the Democratic donkey, the mild little man who represents the American taxpayer, and many others, were born in editorial cartoons and came to be an accepted part of the American scene.

Pictures as well as words are used by our newspapers to explain the news of the world and to influence our attitude toward it.

12.   The Summing up

"The Citizen who is partially informed has no opinions of his own but only the opinions of those who select for him the information he is allowed to have." J. R. Wiggins, Executive Editor of *The Washington Post*.

****

THE MORE COMPLICATED THE WORLD

becomes, the greater are our responsibilities as citizens to understand it. When there are only a few issues, and those are clear-cut, it is easy to make decisions. In the world of today there are thousands of issues, and each one of them is surrounded by as many shades of opinion. Unless our newspapers give us as much of the truth as possible, and unless we read them wisely, we can hardly know what is best. Are our newspapers doing this sort of job for us?

Carl Lindstrom, in *The Disappearing Daily*, calls the American press "A great friendly shaggy pet that wants to play." A. J. Liebling, in *The Wayward Press*, says that to suggest to a publisher that he encourage competition, that he urge his reporters to dig up and print facts which would alienate advertisers, and that he have his editors print editorials that would lose subscribers, would be like telling the owner of a big fat cow to enter it in a horse race.

Some critics insist that because the American press is in business to make money, it cannot be of real service to the public. Most of America's newspapers are business enterprises. They are expensive to buy and expensive to maintain. In a sense they manufacture a product that is different every day (or every edition), that has to please thousands of people of different ages, situations, and tastes, that must be delivered to the public at a certain time, that faces competition which gives almost the same product away free, and that is usually discarded in a few hours. What other manufacturer faces these problems?

William Allen White bought the Emporia *Gazette* in 1892 for $3,000. He estimated that about $750 of the purchase price was for the actual physical assets of the paper. A rotary press, on which most modern newspapers are printed, cost over a million dollars in 1959.

The expenses of a newspaper consist of the plant, the equipment, the raw material, the staff, and the cost of production. All of them have risen astoundingly in the last forty years. According to one estimate, the cost of newsprint alone, the cheap paper on which the news is printed, has risen 230 per cent in this period. One way to keep down the cost of production of a paper is to increase its circulation, because modern methods make it possible to print 40,-000 papers for about the same cost as 20,000. This has resulted in cities with one newspaper instead of several, since one large one can make a profit where several smaller ones will fail.

Critics say that one newspaper in a city will be owned by someone of wealth, who will tend to see all issues from the viewpoint of those who have money. They also say that the monopoly newspaper does not have to improve its quality to beat its competition, but needs only to increase its circulation in order to make a larger profit. Quality in a newspaper means wider and better news coverage and stronger editorial opinions; circulation may be won through contests, entertainment features, and premiums. The first serves the public, the second serves the owner.

The American Newspaper Publishers Association has another viewpoint. It says that in 1961 fifty-nine million copies of newspapers were sold daily in America. Each day Americans bought more newspapers than loaves of bread, bottles of milk, or packs of cigarettes. The Audit Bureau of Circulation figures show that newspaper circulation has more than doubled since 1920, while our population has increased from 105,710,620 to 179,323,175.

Newspaper editors believe that they are publishing more news with less bias than ever before in our history. They point out that the reason for so many newspapers in the past was that they were published to support a particular point of view, and not to make money. A newspaper whose only reason for being is to influence more people to become either Democatrs or Republicans is not as concerned with total news coverage as it is with its own point of view.

A recent public opinion poll showed that more people prefer radio and television as a source of news than newspapers. Does this mean that newspapers are dying? Not according to supporters of the American press. They do not think radio and television can ever supplant the newspaper, because of the nature of the media.

In the early 1930's a few radio stations began the practice of having an announcer read news from a local newspaper over the air. It was felt at the time that perhaps a daily program of this nature, fifteen minutes long, would cover all of the news the average listener could be expected to absorb with his ears.

Today there are hours of daily news broadcasts available on radio and television. These media have their own newsgathering staffs and editors. They provide news coverage impossible for newspapers. They can tell about an event while it is happening and take their listeners to the scene.

The newspaper has the same news, but in greater depth and detail. It provides it in a medium which can be more easily understood. Many details can be heard or seen imperfectly on radio or television, but a news story can be read at leisure and with more complete comprehension.

A newspaper may also be read at the reader's convenience. He must be near a radio or television set at the time the news is being broadcast, and he must listen to all of it in order to hear the portion that interests him most. He may put his paper away to reread later, and he may clip items he wishes to save for further reference. A newspaper also covers events not broadcast on radio or television. Supporters of newspapers say that the habits of Americans in acquiring news may change as the pace of our life changes, but nothing can ever take the place of the newspaper.

The addition of radio and television news coverage has served to improve newspapers by supplying the competition now lacking from other papers in the same vicinity. A newspaper that wished to cover up or distort a particular story would find it impossible because of the other media that are also intent on covering the news.

What about the ambitious young publisher who would like to own his own newspaper, but does not have the money to buy the necessary expensive plant and equipment? Modern technology has made it possible for a young man poorer than William Allen White to set himself up in business.

He does not need to buy his own newspaper plant with expensive presses and other equipment, nor hire an extensive staff to cover the news and pictures.

With the aid of a telephone, a typewriter, an inexpensive camera and a car, he can compile his own paper and have it printed at a large printing press which handles such work. The process of offset printing eliminates the need of expensive metal cuts, and allows pictures to be taken and published the same day. He can take advantage of modern methods of production without owning any of the equipment himself.

Many critics believe that our newspapers do not print enough foreign news, and that facilities for gathering foreign news are inadequate. Publishers counter with the fact that prior to World War I, few Americans were much interested in things that happened outside of our borders and therefore American newspapers carried little such news. An estimated 12 per cent of news space today is devoted to foreign news, and more would be printed if readers were interested.

A. J. Liebling said that the news in American papers is one-sided, since "The Republicans win all of the papers, and the Democrats win all of the elections." In 1964, a leader of the Young Republicans urged members of the group to enter newspaper work so that the viewpoint of that party might offset the preponderance of news slanted from the Democratic viewpoint. It would appear that as long as each party thinks the other controls the press, our newspapers must be giving us both sides.

Newspapers have been widely criticized for sensationalism, for writing stories to attract attention, and for emphasizing much that is wrong in our country. Some people believe that it is better to ignore unpleasant things in the hope that they will disappear, and they see a real danger to our international prestige in the printing of every scandal that happens.

Supporters of our free press say that wrong can be corrected only when it is revealed, and that our citizens can only make the right decisions when they are given all of the facts.

The basic idea behind a free press is that it will act as a check on our government and government officials. We are not surprised to read in a newspaper that one government official has accused another of stupidity and wrong-doing, nor we are dismayed when we read criticisms of our national government and of our President. The more intelligent we are, the more startled we would be *not* to read such news. To thinking people it would be a frightening thing to read day after day that those in power in our country are always right and never make mistakes.

In October 1957 we were disconcerted to read that Russia had put a large satellite in orbit long before we were capable of it. The news was released by the Russian government only after it had been accomplished.

When we made our first attempt, it was covered from beginning to end in our newspapers, and on radio and television. We knew in advance when we were going to try, we knew the names of those involved, and we were given more technical details than we could understand.

The race into space had become a kind of international status symbol and we were aware that a failure on our part would indicate to many peoples of the world that Russia was far ahead of us technically. If her scientists were superior to ours, it might follow in their minds that her way of government was more efficient than ours and potentially more powerful. Some of us criticized the freedom of our press which told the whole world so much about our space program, and revealed our mistakes as well as our ability.

Most of us believe that there is something much more important about our way of life than immediate and popular success. A strong and secure country can afford to let its mistakes be known, and it will not stay strong and secure unless it does. When our newspapers publish details about our national life, they are saying that all of these things belong to us and are our business. The individual citizen's right to know is much more important to a free people than a temporary impression on others.

Stories in an American newspaper about crime, juvenile delinquency, racial discrimination, or corruption in government are not necessarily a sign that democracy is a failure, but perhaps that it is a success. They are a continuing proof that we dare to face the facts about ourselves, and that enough people are interested in what is wrong to try to correct it.

The ultimate fact about the American press is its ownership. As long as it is free to criticize the government, it does not belong to the government. As long as it gives both sides of every question, it does not belong to any one party or faction. As long as it cannot make money for its publishers unless it pleases its readers, it does not belong to the publishers.

The American press belongs, in the long run, to the millions of people who buy its product every day for a few cents, but who will refuse to buy if they do not think it is doing a good job. Since it belongs to us, it is our responsibility to hold its standards high.

For further reading

Adult Titles

COMMITMENT TO FREEDOM (The Story of *The Christian Science Monitor*) by Erwin D. Canham, Houghton, 1958, o.p.

THIS IS LONDON by Edward R. Murrow, Simon & Schuster, 1941, o.p.

COUNTRY EDITOR by Henry Beetle Hough, Doubleday, 1940, o.p.

FOREIGN CORRESPONDENCE: The Great Reporters and Their Times by John Hohenberg, Columbia University Press, 1964

NEWSPAPER DAYS, 1899-1906 by H. L. Menken, Alfred A. Knopf, 1941

FREEDOM OF SPEECH AND PRESS by Edward G. Hudson, Public Affairs, 1962

PORTRAIT OF MYSELF by Margaret Bourke-White (news photographer) Simon & Schuster, 1963

Juvenile Titles

FRONT LINES AND HEADLINES: The Story of Richard Harding Davis by Lewis S. Miner, Messner, 1959

GUARDIANS OF LIBERTY by Olga Hall-Quest, Dutton

TIGER'S TAIL, The Story of Thomas Nast by Nancy Veglahn, Harper, 1964

JOSEPH PULITZER: FRONT PAGE PIONEER by Iris Noble, Messner, 1957

PETER ZENGER: FIGHTER FOR FREEDOM by Tom Galt, Crowell, 1951

PRINTER'S DEVIL TO PUBLISHER (Adolph S. Ochs of *The New York Times*) by Doris Faber, Messner, 1963

THE WONDERFUL WORLD OF COMMUNICATION by Lancelot Hogben, Garden City, 1959

Reference Tools

Ayer's Directory of Newspapers and Periodicals (revised annually)

International Yearbook of *Editor and Publisher* (includes listing of films pertaining to the newspaper business)

The Working Press of the Nation

The Press Intelligence Directory

Index

Biography of Duane Bradley

Duane Bradley was serving as roving reporter for her local newspaper in a small Missouri town at the age of 12. Later she worked on California newspapers for a number of years and is now Henniker correspondent for the *Monitor*, Concord, New Hampshire. She herself exemplifies the qualities of a good newspaper man (or woman) set forth in this book—an active curiosity, a strong faith in the democratic process, and a belief in the right of the people to know the facts about whatever concerns them.

Duane Bradley (Mrs. George Sanborn in private life) was born in Iowa and spent her childhood in the rich farming areas of that state and Missouri, eventually moving to southern California where she worked on newspapers for a number of years.

During World War II she and her family saw more of these United States as her husband's army service assignments took them to Washington, Rhode Island, and Delaware. By the end of the war they had settled in the small New Hampshire town where they now live and from which her husband's family originally came. Her early interest in writing expressed itself in short verses and stories and by her teens she had won a prize in a national short story contest. She has published eight other books for young people.

Her first book for Van Nostrand's juvenile list was ELECTING A PRESIDENT which was selected by the U. S. Information Agency for publication in the Korean language.